# Cambridge Elements

Elements in the Philosophy of Immanuel Kant
edited by
Desmond Hogan
*Princeton University*
Howard Williams
*University of Cardiff*
Allen Wood
*Indiana University*

# KANT AND TELEOLOGY

Thomas Teufel
*The City University of New York*

Shaftesbury Road, Cambridge CB2 8EA, United Kingdom

One Liberty Plaza, 20th Floor, New York, NY 10006, USA

477 Williamstown Road, Port Melbourne, VIC 3207, Australia

314–321, 3rd Floor, Plot 3, Splendor Forum, Jasola District Centre,
New Delhi – 110025, India

103 Penang Road, #05–06/07, Visioncrest Commercial, Singapore 238467

Cambridge University Press is part of Cambridge University Press & Assessment,
a department of the University of Cambridge.

We share the University's mission to contribute to society through the pursuit of
education, learning and research at the highest international levels of excellence.

www.cambridge.org
Information on this title: www.cambridge.org/9781009662383

DOI: 10.1017/9781108529617



When citing this work, please include a reference to the DOI 10.1017/9781108529617

First published 2025

A catalogue record for this publication is available from the British Library

ISBN 978-1-009-66238-3 Hardback
ISBN 978-1-108-43855-1 Paperback
ISSN 2397-9461 (online)
ISSN 2514-3824 (print)

# Kant and Teleology

Elements in the Philosophy of Immanuel Kant

DOI: 10.1017/9781108529617
First published online: March 2025

---

Thomas Teufel
*The City University of New York*

**Author for correspondence:** Thomas Teufel, Thomas.Teufel@baruch.cuny.edu

**Abstract:** Kant's mature teleological philosophy in the *Critique of the Power of Judgment* is predicated on innovations that address a set of unprecedented challenges arising from within critical philosophy. The challenges are (1) a threat of "transcendental chaos" between sensibility and understanding, emerging from the structure of critical epistemology; (2) a threat of "critical chaos" between determination and reflection, generated by Kant's response to that first threat. The innovations include (a) a transcendental conception of purposiveness, (b) a principle of nature's purposiveness based on that conception, (c) a power of judgment governed by that principle, (d) and so governed in an unusual (self-given and self-governing) way, (e) a view on which nature does make leaps. This Element argues that Kant's mature teleological philosophy – and a fortiori Kant's aesthetics and philosophy of biology – cannot be understood without a fully systematic account of these challenges and innovations, and it presents such an account.

**Keywords:** function, organism, purposiveness, reflecting judgment, systematicity



ISBNs: 9781009662383 (HB), 9781108438551 (PB), 9781108529617 (OC)
ISSNs: 2397-9461 (online), 2514-3824 (print)

# Contents

# 1 Kant's Critical Teleology

## 1.1 Introduction: The *Logos* of *Telē*

Teleology is the study (*logos*) of ends (*telē*).[1] It is a branch of learning that dates back to Aristotle, who first made ends (or aims, goals, purposes) amenable to systematic investigation by conceiving of them as a special kind of cause: a *final cause*. Final causes name "that for the sake of which" (Aristotle 1985, 30) a thing is brought into being or the reason why it is there. Appeal to the that-for-the-sake-of-which of a thing explains the coming-into-being of the thing in terms of its propensity to bring about an effect. It thus explains the *thing as effect* in terms of the *effect of the thing*. If this sounds strange, it is! At the heart of all teleology dwells a curious teleological loop, which creates the central conundrum of this fascinating yet confounding science. The *logos* of *telē* is premised on the idea that the cause of a thing and the effect of that thing can – under certain conditions and in certain respects – be the same thing. The term "end" can, accordingly, be used to refer to one, the other, or both.[2]

Perhaps reflective of this unfathomable logic, which conjures the twin specters of backwards causality and self-causation, and in spite of its august and ancient roots, the study of ends remained nameless for centuries, a Frankenstein's monster among philosophy's children and one that is perhaps not incidentally related to the mystery of life. Enlightenment light was shed and the taxonomic embarrassment rectified in 1728, by the great German rationalist and systematizer of all things philosophical Christian Wolff. Remarking in his *Philosophia Rationalis Sive Logica* that the *logos* of *telē* "still lacks a name" (Wolff 1728, 25), Wolff gave the science an unceremonious adult baptism: "It can be called *teleology*" (25).[3]

But naming the beast hardly solved the philosophical problems. The teleological loop is relatively straightforwardly domesticated (if not thereby fully demystified) as it pertains to products of human intelligence, be they words, deeds, or artifacts. Here, the presence of intelligent agency allows us to say that it is not strictly speaking the effect of the thing but the anticipation of the effect

---

[1]  All references to Kant's works, with the exception of those to the *Critique of Pure Reason*, are to Kant (1902–) and are preceded by standard abbreviations (CJ for *Critique of the Power of Judgment*; FI for *First Introduction to the Critique of the Power of Judgment*; CPrR for *Critique of Practical Reason*; JL for *Jäsche Logic*; UTP for *On the Use of Teleological Principles in Philosophy*; Corr for *Correspondence*). Following standard practice, references to the *Critique of Pure Reason* will be to the pagination of the A and B editions. All translations from Kant's works follow (with occasional slight modifications) Kant (1992, 1998, and 2000).

[2]  Even Kant's otherwise rigorous account is not entirely immune to the potential for confusion this creates. On at least three occasions, Kant contradicts his official view – according to which a purpose is the *effect* of a conceptual cause – and refers to that conceptual cause *itself* as the "purpose" (see CJ, 05:180.31–32; FI, 20: 232.16–17; UTP, 08:181.13).

[3]  See McLaughlin (2001, 16n1).

of the thing (usually tied to a desire for the reality of the effect so anticipated) that serves as the cause that helps explain the thing's coming-into-being. To say that the anticipated effect of the game coming on caused me to press the remote, because that typically has the effect of the game coming on, is to give a perfectly respectable teleological explanation of my remote-pressing.

Unfortunately, matters are not quite as straightforward concerning other features of the world that are not (or not in an obvious sense) products of human intentional agency – but to which teleological thinking nevertheless applies with near-equal intuitiveness and inevitability. These include (a) the organization of biological nature, (b) the order and unity of causal powers in nature,[4] (c) the nature and structure of mental phenomena, and (d) the nature and structure of systems of value (e.g., moral or aesthetic).

In the absence of a finite (human) purposing intelligence by means of which to explain these features of the world, the traditional strategy to defang the loop that their teleological explanation incurs was to posit an infinite (divine) purposing intelligence. However, reflexive recourse to speculative theology in matters of science and philosophy fell out of favor in the early modern era.[5] We can see this, for instance, in the gradual move, in the seventeenth and eighteenth centuries, from preformationist to epigenetic theories of biological development. Preformationists sought to minimize divine agency by relegating it to an original act of creation but could explain biological complexity only by making that act vastly complex. Epigeneticists sought to minimize divine agency further by conceding original creation while explaining the development of biological complexity naturally, without appeal to a creator-God.[6] In the same vein, the deistic strategy of invoking a divine artificer in order to render teleological loops innocuous began to lose its appeal as well[7] (a process that was itself far from linear[8]).

Eliminating divine agency from the teleological equation in nonartifactual domains meant that theorists had to naturalize teleology. The conceptual map of naturalized, nondeistic teleology accommodates three broad theoretical strategies: (a) reductive theories that seek to cut through the teleological loop by staying within the causal paradigm that governs the physical sciences, while

---

[4] To be sure, causal laws are not teleological laws (they describe *what* happens, not *why* it happens). But the integration of these laws into a coherent system of scientific knowledge presupposes that the natural world is open to rational inquiry. And that, in turn, is intuitively (and near-inevitably) explained by the broadly teleological idea that nature exhibits rational order. The notion of such rational order is a central theme in Kant's discussion in the Appendix to the Dialectic of the *Critique of Pure Reason* and again in the Introduction of the *Critique of the Power of Judgment* (see Section 3.2).

[5] See Hume (1998).　　[6] See Mensch (2013, chs. 1–2).　　[7] See McDonough (2011, 188).

[8] See McDonough (2020, 167).

allowing that the effect of a thing can nevertheless in some non-self-defeating (noncircular) sense be considered the cause of that thing (contemporary "selected effects" as well as "causal role" theories of biological function fall into this category);[9] (b) nonreductive, neo-Aristotelian, teleological realist theories that embrace the teleological loop by positing a nonmechanistic, teleological form of causality as metaphysically *sui generis* (the *vis essentialis* of proponents of vitalist epigenesis[10] as well as much of the metaphysics of nineteenth-century German Idealism fall into this category); (c) eliminative theories that dismiss the teleological loop by considering teleology as perhaps psychologically necessitated and heuristically expedient but, beyond that, metaphysically groundless ("fictionalist" theories of biological function fall into this category).[11] Contemporary teleological theorizing, especially concerning the functional organization of biological nature, continues to be circumscribed by these broad strategies.

## 1.2 The *Critique of the Power of Judgment*

The central contribution of Kant's mature teleological philosophy in the *Critique of the Power of Judgment* (1790), which shall be the focus of this Element, is to put an additional, nonintentionalist, nondeistic,[12] yet also non-naturalized item on the teleological menu. Kant's solution to the teleological conundrum is distinctly critical and appropriately foundational as he seeks to vindicate teleological thinking as an a priori, necessary, and transcendentally justified form of cognition that is both logically respectable and epistemically indispensable to intellects like ours. He seeks to accomplish this in a three-part maneuver that begins with a subtle yet consequential reconceptualization of traditional teleology in terms of a transcendental-philosophically streamlined

---

[9] See Garson (2016, chs. 3, 5).   [10] See Goy (2017, 333–344).

[11] See Garson (2019, 17–19).

[12] Kant is, of course, deeply interested in questions of rational theology. Kant, moreover, uses his teleological findings in the *Critique of the Power of Judgment* in order to construct an "ethicotheology" (CJ, 5:442.12) in the book's concluding sections on the Methodology of the Teleological Power of Judgment (§§79–91). But while his critical teleology thus "does open up for us a prospect on nature that may perhaps allow us to determine more precisely the otherwise so fruitless concept of an original being" (CJ, 5:437.16–17) – and while it thus "naturally precedes" (CJ, 5:436.11) such a "more precise determination" of that concept – this "moral theology" (CJ, 5:436.08) transcends the proper bounds of Kant's critical teleology. Kant insists that if one understands the "physical teleology" (CJ, 5:442.06) that forms the terminal point of his *teleological* explorations in the third *Critique* in *theological* terms – as a "physicotheology" (CJ, 5:436.04, 5:442.06) – then one has "misunderstood" (CJ, 5:442.06) it. While Kant's argument for his critical teleology supplies materials for theological arguments, it neither starts from theological premises nor reaches theological conclusions. Kant's teleological thought stands independent of his theological thought. But see Goy (2017, 187–188), Guyer (2020, 204).

conception of purposiveness. Next, Kant introduces a transcendental principle based on that conception and identifies it as the principle of a hitherto overlooked cognitive faculty, the reflecting power of judgment. Finally, Kant employs this principle in a theory of a priori reflecting judgments of purposiveness that systematically juxtaposes Kant's own technical with the conventional conception of purposiveness, in the process generating the fundamental subdivision of his critical teleology into a part concerned with aesthetic phenomena and a part concerned with biological phenomena.

The interpretation of Kant's critical teleology advanced in this Element is a novel interpretation. It seeks to breathe new life into Kant's own conception of his critical teleology as highly systematic – both in the internal organization of the *Critique of the Power of Judgment* itself and in its relation to Kant's critical epistemology in the *Critique of Pure Reason*. While an interpretation that takes this systematicity seriously is unusual and faces exegetical and philosophical difficulties that may make the project seem imprudent, the topic of this Element – *Kant and Teleology* – affords an opportunity to confront these challenges and take a fresh look at Kant's critical teleology as an internally coherent and transcendental-logically necessary part of Kant's critical philosophy.

Still, the Element's topic and my approach to it pose special challenges for an introductory text. The philosophical stakes Kant confronts in his critical teleology, as reflected in the various forms of cognitive chaos I discuss in Sections 4.2 and 5.5 (empirical, transcendental, critical), at times make the book operate at a level of abstraction that stretches the bounds of the genre. Need things really be so complicated? Schopenhauer, for one, thought teleology was an exceedingly simple idea and that Kant's treatment of it only exhibited his "peculiar talent for turning an idea about and about . . . until a book has come out of it" (Schopenhauer 1969, 532). I hope to show that Kant's treatment is not so much meandering and convoluted as it is the result of a struggle with genuine philosophical difficulties – and that, despite those difficulties, Kant's eventual solution to the teleological conundrum is, in its own way, simple and ingenious.

### 1.2.1 Backward-Looking and Forward-Looking Dimensions of Teleology

Kant's strategy for making teleology amenable to transcendental-philosophical treatment in the *Critique of the Power of Judgment* is inspired by an old Aristotelian distinction. Kant analyzes the notion of teleology into a backward-looking dimension, concerned with the conceptual cause of a thing (roughly corresponding to Aristotle's *causa formalis*, which determines what sort of thing a conceptually caused object is[13]), and a forward-looking dimension,

---

[13] See CJ, 5:227.17, 23.

concerned with the prospective effect of a thing (roughly corresponding to Aristotle's *causa finalis*, which determines what such a sort of thing is for). Kant notes that only the backward-looking dimension lends itself to transcendental-philosophical analysis because the forward-looking dimension ineliminably depends on empirical determinations (specifically, on the content of conceptually efficacious concepts as well as on the presence of agential aims and desires). Based on this analysis and evaluation, Kant defines his own technical notion of "purposiveness" strictly in terms of the former, backward-looking, etiological conception as "the causality of a concept with respect to its object" (CJ, 5:220.03–04).[14]

Even the backward-looking dimension of teleology is, of course, not entirely free from empirical determinations. To consider a thing's concept its cause appeals to that concept's content and to prospective aims and desires enshrined in it. I cannot explain what sort of thing a hammer is (*causa formalis*) if I cannot explain what it is for (*causa finalis*). This, too, was seen clearly by Aristotle, who cautions in *Physics* II.7 that, despite the theoretical distinction he draws between them, "the what [it is] and that for the sake of which are one" (Aristotle 1985, 30).

Note, however, that, while the backward-looking dimension of teleology is thus empirically inseparable from forward-looking considerations (hence, from questions regarding a causally efficacious concept's content as well as from contingent facts about human agency and desire), Kant's definition of purposiveness considers the central term of art in the *Critique of the Power of Judgment* strictly "according to its transcendental determinations" (CJ, 5:219.31). Kant's aim is to highlight the fact that, despite this empirical inseparability, the backward-looking dimension of conceptual causality is not ineliminably dependent on contingent factors. By abstracting from questions relating to the content of a given formal cause as well as from attendant matters of intention and design, Kant isolates the nonempirical core of the causality of a concept with respect to its object. It consists in the bare metaphysical fact that there must be a representational link, in addition to a causal link, between a causally efficacious concept and its object-cum-effect.[15] Limited to this

---

[14] Kant appeals to this – his official – definition of the term throughout the text of the third *Critique*. See CJ, 5:177.20n., 180.31–34, 307.29–30, 367.01–03, 369.33–35, 372.31–33, 393.31, 408.04–06, 454.23–26; FI, 20:196.18–20, 217.24–27, 230.22–24; see also CPrR, 5:09.2n. See Ginsborg (1997), Teufel (2011a).

[15] To be sure, the forward-looking dimension of conceptual causality – which concerns how a conceptually caused thing in turn engenders its intended effect(s) – also has a nonempirical core and depends on noncontingent factors. But those are not unique to a specifically conceptual form of causality. If we abstract from agential aims and desires and the content of the conceptually caused thing's conceptual cause, then the noncontingent factors of the forward-looking dimension of conceptual causality that remain are just causal. The same is not true of the

foundational feature of conceptual causality, Kant's etiological conception of purposiveness entails an ontological sorting of the world into objects whose concept figured in their causal ancestry and objects whose concept did not. Kant, in short, builds his critical teleology on a transcendental-philosophically purified, formal conception of artifactuality, deliberately freed from substantive, material questions about what a conceptually caused object may be, what it may be for, and whether it succeeds at being so.[16]

That Kant should accord the terminological top spot in his critical teleology to an etiological conception of purposiveness deliberately drained of conventional teleological motifs – hence to formal over final causality – has struck many commentators as problematic: a counterintuitive fact best ignored, discounted, or explained away rather than embraced and elucidated.[17] But there is no deep mystery here. Kant is not wavering on the teleological dimension of teleology. Rather, Kant's project of a duly critical teleology requires a streamlined conception of purposiveness at its heart precisely in order to assert philosophical control over the meanderings of the teleological loop. Specifically, by separating forward-looking and empirical (final) determinations of teleology from backward-looking and nonempirical (formal) determinations, Kant separates descriptive from justificatory contexts and thus delimits the conceptual space within which a proper critique of teleology first becomes possible.

### 1.2.2 Transcendental Teleology

Based on this transcendental-philosophically streamlined conception of purposiveness Kant then proposes a new transcendental principle as the supreme principle of a duly critical teleology, the "[transcendental] principle of the formal purposiveness of nature" (CJ, 5:181.13; or "principle of nature's purposiveness," for short). In simplest terms, the principle of nature's purposiveness demands that finite intelligences like ours approach the world with the assumption that cognizable order resides within it (see Section 4.4.1). This is a principle of formal "purposiveness" because Kant thinks that we cannot conceive of cognizable order except on the model of conceptual order and because he thinks that we cannot conceive of conceptual order residing *in* the world except on the model of artifacts. The idea here is that in the case of artifacts we know that concepts are in a sufficiently thick ontological sense *in* their objects – they in-form or structure their objects – because

---

backward-looking dimension. If we abstract from contingent factors, then the noncontingent factors of the backward-looking dimension of conceptual causality that remain continue to include an ineliminable reference to the presence of a conceptual cause.

[16] See CJ, 5:311.16–20.

[17] See, e.g., Goy (2017, 38n15). In the anglophone world, the tendency is aided by the *Cambridge Edition*'s translation of "*Zweck*" as "end" (see Guyer 2000, xlviii).

they play a representational-cum-causal role in bringing their objects into being. And Kant's technical term for this conceptual inexistence – hence, for the type of causality in which a concept figures in the causal ancestry of its object – is "purposiveness."

Failure to accord Kant's transcendental conception of purposiveness its proper role as *causa formalis* is at the root of the widespread view that the transcendental principle of nature's purposiveness portrays nature finalistically – as purposive *for us*. There are, to be sure, multiple layers of cognitive utility at work in the principle, which play important roles in Kant's presentation: (a) since the counterfactually presumed absence of a principle of nature's formal purposiveness would spell chaos for our form of cognition, its transcendentally deduced presence is commensurately good *for us*; (b) the principle's "demand for an assumption of nature's purposiveness" (see Sections 4.4.5–7) is a heautonomous demand both by and *for us* (namely by and for our reflecting power of judgment); (c) the assumption so demanded represents an isomorphism between intuitive manifolds and concepts that first makes those manifolds cognitively available *for us* (namely for our understanding); (d) transcendentally grounded teleological judgments of organized beings provide heuristic license to treat nature at large as a "system of purposes" (CJ, 5:377.26) of which we are part and that, accordingly, has benefits *for us* (not least in its beautiful products). But it is a terminologically induced oversimplification – predicated on which a transcendental deduction of the principle of nature's purposiveness becomes impossible – to take these attendant or derivative utilities (let alone appeals to foresight or intent) to be part of the content of Kant's principle.

The task of Kant's transcendental deduction of this principle is then to show that the principle's demand for an assumption of nature's purposiveness underlies all forms of theoretical judgment, not just forms of judgment we might consider overtly teleological. Kant, in other words, accords the principle an a priori, necessary, universal, and subpersonal cognitive role as a principle presupposed by all pure and empirical theoretical cognition. Accordingly, the principle is not itself a pure or empirical theoretical cognition. Indeed, the distinctive structure of a demand for an assumption makes the principle of nature's purposiveness different from all other transcendentally necessary principles in Kant's critical philosophy. Neither a principle of reason nor a pure principle of the understanding, it is identified by Kant as the principle of a hitherto overlooked cognitive faculty, the "reflecting power of judgment" (CJ, 5:180.05).

### 1.2.3 A Priori Reflecting Judgments of Purposiveness

The central if largely unheralded philosophical mechanism – or, perhaps more fittingly, the animating principle – of Kant's *Critique of the Power of Judgment* is that the principle of nature's purposiveness, which finds universal employment at the subpersonal level, also leaves a conscious signature in certain empirical contexts. In those contexts, the principle's standing subpersonal demand for an assumption of nature's purposiveness becomes phenomenally manifest as the sense that a sensibly given object originated in its concept and, a fortiori, that there is a way it is supposed to be (as fixed by the concept so presumed). The unconventional idea at the heart of Kant's critical teleology is that, even as it thus attaches directly to an empirical object, the principle's demand for an assumption of nature's purposiveness remains empirically – but not, therefore, transcendental-logically – ungrounded. The principle's demand here accordingly registers as a quasi-auratic sense of the object's artifactuality – a feeling of being unaccountably compelled to consider it as "of conceptual origin."[18] Notably, this sense is independent of the object's actual provenance and may attach to products of human ingenuity as much as to products of nature. The peculiar form of judgment in and through which the principle's demand for an assumption of nature's inexistent order thus comes to be applied to empirical objects, occasioning the feeling in question, is the principal philosophical vehicle for the doctrines of Kant's critical teleology: an a priori reflecting judgment of purposiveness.

The claim that, at the structural core of the third *Critique*, we find a form of a priori judgment that applies only to select individuals situated in certain empirical contexts, that is not determined by observable features of the objects in question, and whose signature attribution of purposiveness consequently conveys an ineffable sense of these objects' artifactuality will sound surprising to the reader familiar with the literature on Kant's third *Critique*. For one thing, the apriority of reflecting judgments is often treated as a peculiarity of Kant's aesthetics – where, for good structural reasons, it is on fuller display than in Kant's teleology – rather than as the key to the *Critique of the Power of Judgment* as a whole. For another, this apriority is typically not treated as a characteristic of first-order reflecting judgments at all; not because that is not Kant's position but because – in the absence of a fully systematic account of Kant's critical teleology – it is hard to explain how it can be Kant's position.

That the importance and role of a priori reflecting judgments of purposiveness has traditionally been miscast has to do with a delicate hermeneutic

---

[18] Walter Benjamin's concept of "*Aura*" (Benjamin 1991, 438) is useful in this context because the sense of artifactuality at issue attaches to spatiotemporally *determinate* individuals, despite being perceptually and conceptually *in*determinate – it names an atmosphere, not a feature. Unlike Benjamin's "aura," however, this sense is not a mysterious, spiritual emanation we "breathe" ("*die Aura ... atmen*"; Benjamin 1991, 440) but a duly transcendental-logically backed form of awareness. Reminiscent of Benjamin's evanescent phenomenon, yet cognitively more robust, I accordingly consider it quasi-auratic.

difficulty that must be addressed up front. From the perspective of the *Critique of Pure Reason* – and, in general, within a logical framework whose paradigm case of judgment is predicative (i.e., determining) judgment – the combination of epistemic apriority, transcendental necessity, logical singularity, and quasi-auratic predicative holism that characterizes a priori reflecting judgments of purposiveness appears to be fully – and flagrantly – inconsistent.[19,20] According to that paradigm, epistemically a priori and transcendentally necessary judgments can only be logically universal, not logically singular judgments.[21] What they say applies to all or, failing that, to no objects; but not to some (and not to others). To make matters worse, the proposed phenomenal manifestation of these a priori-yet-singular reflecting judgments of purposiveness (namely an empirically ungrounded sense of their objects' artifactuality) cannot but sound unduly esoteric to Kantian ears and so appear to be well beyond the critical-philosophical pale. If, by the lights of the *Critique of Pure Reason*, the price of admission to Kant's *Critique of the Power of Judgment* requires payment in illogical and uncritical coin, then that, surely, is not the show we came to see.

As a result, interpreters often try, incongruously, to retrofit Kant's systemic innovations in the third *Critique* with the more comforting conventions governing "the land of pure understanding" (A 235/B 294) from whose shores Kant's *Critique of the Power of Judgment* so intrepidly cuts loose (following a somewhat bungled maiden voyage in the Appendix to the Transcendental Dialectic in the first *Critique*, of which more in Section 3.2.1). Even employing this inverted heuristic, admirable sense can still be made of some of the doctrines of the third *Critique*. But we cannot truly understand what Kant is trying to teach us about the reflecting power of judgment, its a priori principle, the a priori reflecting judgments that principle governs, and, most importantly, the broadly teleological (aesthetic and biological) phenomena those judgments seek to capture if, guided by a desire for safe passage, we misread reflection as a form of determination.[22]

Nor are the consequences of the hermeneutically sounder approach of casting off alongside Kant and meeting the *Critique of the Power of Judgment* on its own terms as dire as feared. First, there are sound structural considerations that make the transcendental principle of nature's purposiveness a philosophical

---

[19] For the characteristic of epistemic apriority, see CJ, 5:193.25–27, 194.15–17; for transcendental necessity, see CJ, 5:288.14–20; for logical singularity, see CJ, 5:288.14–20; for quasi-auratic predicative holism, see CJ, 5:314.32–33, 377.10–13.

[20] See Beck (1978, 169).     [21] See B 4.

[22] The "inverted heuristic" involves a cluster of related misreadings that include interpreting a priori reflecting judgments of purposiveness (a) as a posteriori judgments, (b) on the model of concept-forming syntheses, (c) as concerned with final causes, and (d) as primarily object-directed as opposed to self-given (autonomous) and self-governing (heautonomous) cognitions.

necessity within Kant's critical epistemology (see Sections 4.3.2 and 4.4.1–2) and that make the a priori-yet-singular reflecting judgments of purposiveness that derive from that principle consistent with logic and transcendental logic alike (see Sections 5.4.4 and 5.5). Second, scary talk of auras may lose some of its immediate terror when we consider a fundamental truth from the philosophy of biology that sometimes gets lost in contemporary debates about biological functions: functional relations are not observationally accessible – but they are not imaginary either. Kant's theory of a priori reflecting judgments of purposiveness is deeply committed to and expressive of that truth. In a pivotal passage, Kant puts the matter this way: "the purposiveness of a thing, insofar as it is *presented in perception*, is not a property of the object itself (since such a property *cannot be perceived*)" (CJ, 5:189.21–22, my emphases). We do not perceive a biological trait's for-the-sake-of-ness – but we necessarily judge the trait to exhibit it. The idea of *imperceptibilia* in perception reflects Kant's basic critical outlook that "all our cognition commences *with* experience, yet it does not on that account all arise *from* experience" (B 1). As applied here, the outlook suggests that judging a biological trait teleologically is entirely nonoptional. A trait would not be a *trait* – an organ would not be an *organ* – if we did not antecedently (and, in the absence of observational access, nonempirically) frame it in functional terms.

Despite an undeniable reimagining of the critical framework in response to unprecedented challenges from within – specifically, (a) a threat of "transcendental chaos" between sensibility and understanding (see Section 4.2.3) and, as a consequence of the critical-philosophical response to that first threat, (b) a subsequent threat of "critical chaos" between reflection and determination (see Section 5.5) – and despite a considerable degree of philosophical daring exhibited in the process, Kant's third *Critique* is, at bottom, a conservative book, one that seeks to complete rather than to undo critical philosophy.

### 1.2.4 Transcendental and Empirical Dimensions of Teleology

If a priori reflecting judgments of purposiveness are the principal vehicles for the aesthetic and biological doctrines of Kant's *Critique of the Power of Judgment*, then how do they work? As noted, the peculiarity of these judgments is that, despite the apriority of their attribution of purposiveness, they are logically singular first-order judgments or judgments that attribute purposiveness only to select individuals situated in certain empirical contexts. Setting aside the central question how these epistemic and logical characteristics can possibly coexist in the same cognitive structure and how the structure that unites them comes to be in the first place (see the discussion of nature's *saltūs* in Sections 2.2.4 and 5.4.4), their surprising combination sets up a potent tension that is determinative of the aforementioned cognitive signature. For, while these judgments are not determined by observable features of their objects (on account of their apriority), they are nevertheless subject to empirical constraints (on account of their logical singularity). Principally, they are subject to a determination whether the sense of their object's purposiveness – as conveyed by the a priori attribution of an origin in its concept to it – can be empirically satisfied.

Depending on whether the sense of the object's purposiveness can be empirically satisfied, the a priori reflecting judgment expressing it is then either an a priori reflecting judgment of a (transcendental) purposiveness without (empirical) purpose or an a priori reflecting judgment of a (transcendental) purposiveness with (empirical) purpose. This contextual sorting of a priori reflecting judgments of purposiveness into a variety without and another with (empirical) purpose is foundational to the third *Critique* – it is the rationale behind the subdivision of Kant's book into two parts, aesthetic and teleological, that, on the surface, share little else in common.

Much of the conceptual power of Kant's critical teleological philosophy is due to his adept navigation of the intersection between transcendental-philosophically separable yet empirically inseparable aspects of teleological thinking. For, in empirical contexts, the "what-it-is" (*causa formalis*) and the "that-for-the-sake-of-which" (*causa finalis*) are, as per Aristotle, one. Accordingly, in empirical contexts, the sense that an object originated in its concept, as conveyed by an a priori reflecting attribution of purposiveness to it, is accompanied by an inevitable – but not similarly transcendentally grounded – sense of a goal thereby pursued.

In the case of a priori reflecting judgments of a (transcendental) purposiveness without (empirical) purpose, neither the sense of the object's conceptual origin (what-it-is) nor the accompanying sense of a goal thereby pursued (that-for-the-sake-of-which) can be empirically supported. The consequent tension between our a priori and our a posteriori estimation of the thing is, ex hypothesi, unresolvable. The result is a distinct mix of cognitive and emotive reverberations (the famous "pleasure in the harmony of the faculties of cognition"; CJ, 5:218.10) that ultimately marks this case as aesthetic.

In the case of a priori reflecting judgments of a (transcendental) purposiveness with (empirical) purpose, both the sense of the object's conceptual origin (what-it-is) and the accompanying sense of a goal (that-for-the-sake-of-which) can be empirically supported (if not, thereby, determinatively grounded). The result is an attendant teleological loop: here the empirically available response to the "what-it-is" (what a given biological trait is and does) answers, moreover, to the "that-for-the-sake-of-which" (what that biological trait is supposed to be and do). In nonartifactual domains, this marks the object of such a judgment as a "natural purpose" (CJ, 5:370.31): a nonartifactual, natural object that is and does what it is supposed to be and do – an organic being.

In these two ways, Kant's critical teleology controls the teleological loop. First, in the aesthetic case, the structure of an a priori reflecting judgment of a (transcendental) purposiveness without (empirical) purpose does not invite the loop. Second, in the biological case, the structure of an a priori reflecting judgment of a (transcendental) purposiveness with (empirical) purpose renders the teleological loop it entails philosophically harmless by revealing it as a consequence of our inability to separate transcendentally necessitated from empirical determinations in reflecting attributions of purposiveness – an empirical-psychological free rider of those attributions in those contexts.

This does more than take the teleological loop from vertiginous to vacuous in nonartifactual domains. The structure of an a priori reflecting judgment of a (transcendental) purposiveness with (empirical) purpose takes the loop from vacuous to virtuous. Freed from the need for a transcendental justification of our merely empirical-psychologically inescapable penchant for invoking ends, we can here claim that penchant as a heuristic benefit. Teed up by the reflecting power of judgment, the faculty of reason now takes the lead and interprets our appeal to ends in these transcendentally necessitated reflecting judgments as a heuristic clue in order to judge their objects further – in light of it. If we must judge certain natural objects teleologically on nonempirical grounds in a priori reflecting judgments of purposiveness, then we rationally may judge other empirically accessible features (as well as other empirically given objects) teleologically as well – so long as this proves explanatorily fruitful and does not contradict scientific findings elsewhere.[23] In consequence, teleology comes to be seen as foundational and pervasive. Indeed, the realm of observationally accessible features of the empirical, causal-mechanistic world begins to appear subordinate to teleological considerations – a line of thought explored in Kant's "physical teleology" (CJ, 5:442.06) in the Method of the third *Critique*.

In terms of the earlier conceptual map of nondeistic solutions to the teleological conundrum, we can now locate Kant's own nonintentionalist yet also nonnaturalized solution as follows. Kant neither cuts through nor embraces nor dismisses the teleological loop. Instead, he first lifts the debate from an uncritical, dogmatic level to a transcendental-justificatory level, at which the matter arguably must be addressed. He then evades the teleological loop by means of an incisive conceptual distinction, construing teleological thinking at the transcendental level in terms of his linear, technical definition of "purposiveness."

---

[23]  See CJ, 5:380.26–381.03.

This, furthermore, allows Kant to neutralize the teleological loop at the empirical level, especially in nonartifactual domains, without declaring teleology fictional altogether. This, finally, enables Kant to utilize and promote teleological thinking as a well-motivated heuristic strategy in those domains.

## 2 Philosophy of Biology or Critique of Judgment?

### 2.1 Introduction: The Black Box

The view I present in this Element identifies Kant's critical teleology with Kant's *Critique of the Power of Judgment* at large. The reason for this identification is that the transcendental principle Kant introduces in the *Critique of the Power of Judgment* and that governs virtually all aspects of Kant's book – the transcendental "principle of the formal purposiveness of nature" (CJ, 5:181.13) – is a fundamentally teleological principle. To understand Kant's critical teleology, on this view, is to understand the fortunes of the transcendental principle of nature's purposiveness in the *Critique of the Power of Judgment*. This calls for a systematic approach. We cannot understand the fortunes of the principle of nature's purposiveness unless we understand: (a) the definition of the concept of purposiveness "in accordance with its transcendental determinations" (CJ, 5:219.31) that this principle is based on; (b) the "deduction" (CJ, 5:184.22) that marks the principle based on that conception as a duly transcendental principle; (c) the cognitive role of the "reflecting power of judgment" (CJ, 5:180.05) that this transcendental principle governs; (d) the "reflecting judgments" (CJ, 5:191.21) of beautiful things and organized beings that flow from that power.

The view I present in this Element accordingly does not identify Kant's critical teleology narrowly with Kant's "Critique of the Teleological Power of Judgment" (CJ, 5:357.04–06), in which Kant presents his critical philosophy of biology and which forms the "Second Part" (CJ, 5:357.03) of the *Critique of the Power of Judgment*. This might seem counterintuitive. How can Kant's critical teleology not be the same as Kant's teleological critique? But this way of putting the matter is misleading. Naturally, Kant's critical philosophy of biology is essential to Kant's critical teleology (see Section 2.4). But not much good can come from approaches that either reverse the explanatory order and seek to understand the principles of Kant's critical teleology in terms of Kant's philosophy of biology[24] or carve out Kant's philosophy of biology as a stand-alone teleological doctrine that relates to Kant's systematic investigation of purposiveness in the *Critique of the Power of Judgment* only along the margins.[25]

---

[24] See Goy and Watkins (2014, 8).   [25] See Goy (2017, 224).

Still, a view that identifies Kant's critical teleology narrowly with Kant's philosophy of biology is not easily dismissed. Kant himself does not call his critique of judgment at large a "teleology" in the *Critique of the Power of Judgment* and the broad conception of Kant's critical teleology defended here is hardly the first conception that suggests itself.[26] In the present section, I describe the recommended systematic approach in broad strokes, starting with the elements of Kant's critical teleology and their interaction and ending with two central objections to my view.

Addressing these matters will teach us a lot about the underlying structure of Kant's *Critique of the Power of Judgment*. Kant, it must be said, does not do nearly enough to make the basic shape and animating principle of this structure explicit. On the one hand, he offers a scattered and evolving set of largely implicit rationales for the transcendental status of the principle governing the reflecting power of judgment. On the other hand, he discusses only the cognitive fruits – aesthetic and biological – that power yields. Along the way, Kant offers no explicit account of how the transcendental principle governing that power connects with those fruits. The third *Critique*, in short, is something of a black box, with a transcendental principle of the reflecting power of judgment (and whatever that principle may be exercised on) as input and two kinds of reflecting judgment (aesthetic and teleological) as output.

To make matters worse, Kant fails to provide either unambiguous definitions of key technical terms (e.g., "reflecting" and "regulative") or unambiguous guidelines for his use of unambiguously defined technical terms (e.g., "purposiveness"), leaving the precise nature and significance of the governing principle of reflection and of the resulting reflecting judgments even more uncertain. Factor in that, in purely structural terms, the transcendental principle of nature's purposiveness makes a highly complex demand (which determines the reflecting power of judgment) for an assumption (which determines the determining power of judgment) – concerned, moreover, with ostensibly non-aesthetic and non-biological matters – and whatever may be going on inside that box begins to look unfathomable.

Commentators, it seems, may be excused for favoring the undeniably juicy aesthetic and biological bits over the quite possibly hopeless systematics.[27] But that approach is not only destined to miss what is important – almost by necessity mistaking surface features for inner workings – it is also uncalled for. Kant in fact leaves plenty of clues concerning the underlying structure and

---

[26] Although he explicitly conceived of his third installment of critical philosophy as a "teleology" (Corr, 10:515.02) in the famous letter to Carl Leonhard Reinhold from December 1787 in which he announces the third *Critique*.

[27] But see Ginsborg (2015), Zuckert (2007).

animating principle of the third *Critique*. While there is an indisputable dearth of explicit doctrine addressing that structure and principle – whence they cannot simply be read off the pages of the book – attention to detail, coupled with a synoptic approach to the text, reveals them as simple but ingenious ways of mustering the resources of critical philosophy to account for a set of phenomena that only a few years earlier Kant had deemed beyond its reach.[28]

## 2.2 Elements of Kant's Critical Teleology

Perhaps the most compelling reason for identifying Kant's teleology narrowly with Kant's philosophy of biology is furnished by Kant's subdivision of the third *Critique* itself. Kant divides the book into two parts, a "Critique of the Aesthetic Power of Judgment" (CJ, 5:201.04–06), concerned, principally, with questions of artistic and natural beauty, and a "Critique of the Teleological Power of Judgment" (CJ, 5:357.04–06), concerned, principally, with questions in the philosophy of biology. Both are preceded by a lengthy "Introduction" (CJ, 5:171.01) that discusses ostensibly unrelated and arcane systematic matters (such as the unity of the critical system, the nature of judgment, and the necessity of empirical causal laws).[29] This subdivision gives rise to the entirely natural impression that Kant's third *Critique* is composed of an "aesthetics" and a "teleology," where the latter amounts to Kant's teleology sensu stricto and coincides with Kant's philosophy of biology, give or take. Based on this impression, readers of these pages may reasonably expect a volume on *Kant and Teleology* to be centered around Kant's philosophy of biology.

One may counter this impression by noting that, in Kant's usage, the Greek-rooted German term *Teleologie* refers only to a special kind of purposiveness (exhibited primarily by biological organisms). At least on the surface, then, the German *Zweckmäßigkeit* (purposiveness) – together with its cognates *zweckmäßig* (purposive) and *Zweck* (purpose) – appears to be the governing teleological concept of the third *Critique*. And yet Kant's treatment of distinct phenomena under the broader heading of *Zweckmäßigkeit* could be reflective of a unity in name only. It would then make sense to take the terminological fact that Kant counts only nonartifactual, natural (and, in the first place, biological) phenomena as properly falling within the scope of a "teleology" (CJ, 5:361.01) as the decisive textual clue and accordingly consider only his philosophy of biology and not his *Critique of the Power of Judgment* at large as his teleology proper.

---

[28] See UTP, 8:182.16–20; see also Guyer (2000, xiii–xxi).

[29] Excerpts from an earlier draft of the introduction were first published in 1794, further complicating matters. The draft was published in *toto* in 1914. See FI; see also Guyer (2000, xlii–xliii).

Let us consider the matter more closely. Kant distinguishes between his aesthetics and his teleology in the following, straightforward manner. Kant's aesthetics (the "First Part of the Critique of the Power of Judgment"; CJ, 5:201.01–03) investigates reflecting judgments that diagnose a "purposiveness without purpose" (CJ, 5:226.27–28). Kant's teleology (the "Second Part of the Critique of the Power of Judgment"; CJ, 5:357.01–03) investigates reflecting judgments that diagnose a "purposiveness with purpose."[30] In order to see if there is fundamental unity to Kant's exploration of a variety of forms of purposiveness in the third *Critique*, we must, accordingly, begin with a closer look at: (a) Kant's notion of "purposiveness" (see Section 2.2.1), (b) the idea of "a priori judgments of purposiveness" (see Sections 2.2.2–4), (c) Kant's notion of "purpose" (2.2.5), (d) the idea of judgments of a "purposiveness without purpose" as well as of judgments of a "purposiveness with purpose" (see Section 2.2.6), (e) the fate of the teleological loop in those judgments (see Section 2.2.7).

### 2.2.1 The Causality of Concepts

According to Kant's official definition of the central term of art in the third *Critique*, purposiveness is "the causality of a concept with respect to its object" (CJ, 5:220.03–04). This form of causality differs from mere efficient, mechanistic causality because it posits a causal link as well as a representational link between a concept (as cause) and an object (as effect). The possessive pronoun in Kant's definition emphasizes this duality: conceptual causality is the causal relation between a concept and not any old but *its* object.

Crucially, Kant is interested in this form of causality according to its "transcendental determinations" (CJ, 5:219.31). Whatever may be the justification for a judgment of purposiveness in this transcendental sense (see Section 2.2.4), a judgment of purposiveness in this sense is not concerned with empirical aspects of the causal efficacy of concepts. Such empirical aspects encompass three broad considerations: (a) the content of the causally efficacious concept in question, (b) estimations of the degree to which the object caused satisfies normative constraints placed on it by that causally efficacious concept's content (including the degree to which it accommodates practical uses specified therein), and (c) the aims behind the production of an object of such specification and use (including psychological laws governing this form of production). What matters, instead, for Kant's transcendental definition of purposiveness is the metaphysical fact that in any case of conceptual causality there must *be* a representational, in addition to a causal, link between the causally efficacious concept and *its* object. From Kant's transcendental perspective, it is indifferent

---

[30]  See CJ, 5:359.14–16, 370.33–37.

what that link may be, how we may know it, how strong it may be, or why one would care to exploit it. As a matter of contingent fact, we consider concepts causally efficacious only when situated in the context of agential desires, aims, and intentions, where the questions just intimated matter deeply. But that, according to Kant, is an accident of our human form of agency and mindedness. It is not an essential feature of a concept's purported role as a cause. Transcendental-philosophically, all that matters for a concept to be considered causally efficacious qua concept is that it be not only *causally* linked to *an* object but *representationally* linked to *its* object.

This transcendental-philosophical perspective is central to Kant's nonintentionalist, nondeistic, yet nonnaturalized teleology in two ways. First, by identifying matters of intention, design, and utility as empirical determinations of conceptual causality, Kant separates descriptive from justificatory contexts in the study of teleology. The distinction between *quaestio facti* and *quaestio juris* is, of course, a familiar one in Kant's critical philosophy. In the third *Critique*, it is central in Kant's response to both the traditional design argument and the eliminativist backlash to it, because it allows Kant to treat of the teleological loop without either appealing to a divine artificer or declaring teleology illusory altogether (see Section 2.2.7). Second, by drawing a strict distinction between two kinds of objects – those with and those without purported concepts in their causal ancestry – Kant carves out a special ontological realm of artifactuality within his theoretical philosophy. In the context of the third *Critique*, this is a central element in Kant's response to naturalistic and reductive approaches to teleology, because it allows him to introduce a class of objects for the explanation of which causal mechanism proves universally necessary but not universally sufficient (see Section 5.5).

### 2.2.2 Reflection, Apriority, Singularity

The most perplexing, important, and arguably least well-understood feature of Kant's aesthetics and teleology is that reflecting judgments of purposiveness are at bottom a priori judgments, derivative of the subpersonal cognitive function of the transcendental principle of nature's purposiveness. That is to say, whatever else they may be, reflecting judgments of purposiveness are not, at bottom, a posteriori contemplations of perceptually salient features of empirically given objects, even as they do have important empirical dimensions.

To be sure, the idea that, for Kant, "reflecting" in the third *Critique* names a form of a posteriori contemplation is prephilosophically intuitive and commensurately widespread among commentators. But the idea faces a serious problem. To put it simply: *that* type of reflection is a form of determination. Kant considers any form of deliberative contemplation – whether it stands in the service of determining

objects or in the service of determining concepts – a form of conceptual determination. This very much includes the logical acts involved in empirical concept-
formation – "comparing, reflecting, and abstracting" (JL, 9:94.28–29) – with which
Kant's notion of "reflecting judgment" in the third *Critique* is typically associated.[31]

Perhaps the least appreciated among the principal doctrinal innovations of the
*Critique of the Power of Judgment* is that Kant distinguishes between two kinds of
reflection: one tangential, one central to his critical teleology. The first kind of
reflection is the logical act of "finding the universal for the particular that is
offered to it by perception" (CJ, 5:186.10–11). The task of this kind of reflection is
pedestrian: it is an ex post facto form of deliberation that allows us to form or
refine empirical concepts. Logical reflection arrives at further conceptualizations
of perceptually given and already conceptually determined empirical objects.
Consistent with Kant's pre- and post-third-*Critique* views, his position in the third
*Critique* is that this kind of reflection is the job of the faculty of concepts: it is "the
necessary business of the understanding" (CJ, 5:186.9–10). It is not the business
of the reflecting power of judgment with which the third *Critique* is concerned.

The second kind of reflection is the identical-seeming but fully separate
transcendental-logical act of "ascending from the particular in nature to the
universal" (CJ, 5:180.06). The task of this kind of reflection is rarefied: it is an
a priori and transcendentally necessary cognitive posture that "provides [deter-
minability] for [nature's] supersensible substratum" (CJ, 5:196.15–18).[32] Such
reflection does not proceed from already conceptually determined particular
empirical objects to further empirical conceptualizations of those same objects.
Instead, it ascends from an original state of cognitively untouched particularity
"as such" to a realm of conceptual universality "as such" (see Sections 4.3.2 and
4.4.2).[33] This ascent, Kant explains, is the "obligation" (CJ, 5:180.07) of the new
reflecting power of judgment. Crucially, this a priori kind of reflection, pitched at
that rarefied transcendental-logical level, is at work also in reflecting aesthetic and
reflecting teleological judgments, which flow from that power.

---

[31] Longuenesse (1998, 163–166), Allison (2001, 18), Guyer (2005, 12), Ginsborg (2006), Zuckert
(2007, 69–76).

[32] See CJ, 5:346.15–18.

[33] This a priori "ascent to the universal" is also distinct from Kant's "transcendental reflection" in
the first *Critique*, "through which I distinguish whether [representations] are to be compared with
one another as belonging to the pure understanding or to pure intuition" (A261/B317). *That* form
of reflection is the philosopher's methodological tool for arriving at the analyses and proofs
characteristic of transcendental critique. Such reflection – perhaps suitably modified into
a broader form of "epistemic reflection" (see Westphal, 2004, 17–18) to address philosophical
needs exceeding those of the Transcendental Analytic of the *Critique of Pure Reason* – is
required also for the analyses and proofs of the third *Critique*. But the form of reflection thus
needed to discover and justify the reflecting power of judgment and its principle, while, like all
cognition, dependent on that power, is not itself an exercise of it.

Both a priori and a posteriori kinds of reflection are essential to cognition. Both, moreover, join in the systematization of empirical concepts and laws (an effort guided by heuristic principles that are in turn grounded in the principle of the reflecting power of judgment).[34] However, if, from the start, we misidentify Kant's a priori reflecting judgments in the third *Critique* as a variety of a posteriori determining judgments, then we stand little chance of understanding what Kant may be trying to teach us about aesthetic and biological phenomena by means of the new reflecting power of judgment, its transcendental principle, and the judgments that flow from it.

But taking the apriority of reflecting judgments of purposiveness seriously requires us to unravel a thorny philosophical problem we may not have realized was ours. After all, despite their apriority, reflecting aesthetic judgments of purposiveness (paradigmatically, "this is beautiful") and reflecting teleological judgments of purposiveness (paradigmatically, "this is an organism") very much function like a posteriori judgments. They are singular judgments of select, perceptually given, and conceptually determined empirical objects. How logically singular, ostensibly epistemically a posteriori, and ostensibly metaphysically contingent judgments can – instead and in fact – be epistemically a priori and transcendentally necessary judgments is the central exegetical problem posed by Kant's aesthetics and teleology.[35]

This, too, is not how the matter is typically portrayed in the literature. Lewis White Beck, in "On the Putative Apriority of Judgments of Taste,"[36] emphatically rejects the idea that the apriority of reflecting judgments of purposiveness (and, specifically, of reflecting aesthetic judgments of purposiveness) is a problem for – let alone *the* problem of – the third *Critique*. Beck insists that Kant is "led . . . astray" (Beck 1978, 168) by a "confusion" (167) when he calls such judgments a priori.[37]

Now, according to Kant, "It is an empirical judgment that I perceive and judge an object with pleasure. It is, however, an *a priori* judgment that I find it beautiful, i.e., that I may require that satisfaction of everyone as necessary" (CJ, 5:289.26–29). This programmatic declaration – the last thing Kant says about these judgments before heading into the official "Deduction of Judgments

---

[34] See Teufel (2017, 122–123).

[35] To be sure, variations of this problem have long been discussed in the literature in the form of the worry that Kant seems committed to the notion that everything is beautiful or that everything is organized. But these worries do not typically result from recognition of the apriority of *first*-order reflecting judgments but stem, instead, from interpretations of the role the *second*-order principle of the reflecting power of judgment plays in serving as an a priori ground of those first-order judgments (which, themselves, are deemed to be a posteriori).

[36] See Beck (1978).

[37] Paul Guyer calls Kant's paragraph "clumsy" (Guyer 1997, 231); Henry Allison calls Kant's language "misleading" (Allison 2001, 174).

of Taste" (CJ, 5:289.31) – is consistent with Kant's position throughout: reflecting judgments of purposiveness are a priori judgments.[38] Still, in Beck's telling, Kant's clear-cut pronouncement is anything but. According to Beck's reconstruction, Kant mistakenly attributes the apriority characteristic of the second-order principle of reflection – by which I am entitled to "require that satisfaction of everyone as necessary" – to first-order reflecting aesthetic judgments themselves. That I am entitled to require satisfaction of everyone in a judgment of taste is a priori; that I require it in a given case surely is not.

The professed reason for Beck's intervention is that any apriority of first-order reflecting aesthetic judgments would preclude the possibility of errors of taste: "they could hardly be *a priori but erroneous*" (Beck 1978, 169; emphasis Beck). But this only begs Kant's question. A priori judgments cannot be erroneous. But we can be mistaken about whether our judgments are a priori in the first place precisely if they are, moreover, "singular judgments of specific cases" (169). This is most apparent in the aesthetic case, where my only indication of the due apriority of my judgment is a set of cognitively rooted but highly fallible feelings (specifically, a quasi-auratic sense of an object's purposiveness and a related awareness of the disinterestedness of my pleasure in that object).[39]

The true reason for Beck's intervention is logical incredulity: qua "singular judgments of specific cases" reflecting aesthetic judgments simply cannot be a priori! And, just like that, Beck puts the problem of the apriority of first-order reflecting judgments to rest for modern third-*Critique* scholarship, so much so that commentators, expanding on Beck's reconstruction, can soon retire the unseemly charge of confusion and maintain that Kant either never meant to[40] or

---

[38] See CJ, 5:193.25–27, 194.16–17, 218.25, 288.22–23, 376.17–22.

[39] This, moreover, is why there is a need for a "Deduction of Judgments of Taste" (CJ, 5:289.31), not mirrored in Kant's philosophy of biology, despite the fact that the apriority of the attribution of purposiveness in a reflecting judgment of a "purposiveness without purpose" is a structural given. For, in the absence of a "purpose," the a priori attribution of purposiveness, whether to a nonpurposive, natural object or to a purposive, artifactual object, triggers an open-ended empirical-psychological engagement of my cognitive faculties that seeks to reconcile the inevitable tension (on either scenario) between my transcendental and my empirical estimation of the thing (see Section 2.2.6). This "free play" (CJ, 5:217.22) of the faculties registers as a form of cognitive and a fortiori nondesirous or disinterested pleasure in the (judging of the) object. A full-fledged judgment of taste is the expression of this pleasure, notable for its implicit demand that any similarly positioned observer, too, respond with that satisfaction. Qua feeling, and despite its disinterested quality, this satisfaction must, however, be subjective and private. It is thus prima facie not the sort of thing I rightfully *can* demand of others; unless the cognitive engagement that elicits it in me can be presumed the same in all. Kant's deduction says it can.

[40] See Guyer (1997, 231).

even that he never did[41] propose the apriority of first-order reflecting judgments to begin with.[42] The order of the critical universe is thus preserved, but only at the expense of first labeling the Sage of Königsberg's commitment to the apriority of first-order reflecting judgments of purposiveness befuddled – and then politely escorting that commitment off the stage.

### 2.2.3 A Statement of Purpose

The present interpretation takes the opposite tack: No systematic interpretation of Kant's mature teleological philosophy can afford to ignore or long escape Kant's foundational commitment to the apriority of first-order reflecting judgments of purposiveness. The doctrine captures how the self-given self-governance of the transcendental principle of nature's purposiveness opens access to a world of beauty and biological organization for intellects like our own. It is the beating heart and the raison d'être – the "what-it-is" and "that-for-the-sake-of-which" – of Kant's mature teleology in the *Critique of the Power of Judgment*.

Consider, by way of instructive contrast, Kant's pre-third-*Critique* theoretical philosophy. According to Kant's earlier views, judgments of beauty are transcendental-logically unwarranted subjective expressions of pleasure in an object;[43] judgments of biological (functional) organization are transcendental-logically unwarranted, if rationally expedient, analogical responses to natural complexity – useful teleological fictions.[44] Nor could there be categorially grounded determining judgments of taste or teleology. While such judgments would treat the phenomena in question as appropriate targets of empirical-scientific investigation, they would eo ipso flout those targets' distinctive nature as phenomena of beauty and biology. Caught between the Scylla of subjectivity and fictionality and the Charybdis of objectivity and disenchantment, Kant has little choice but to opt for the former in addressing the aesthetic and biological dimensions of the human experience. Rather than explain those dimensions, however, this shortchanges them and exposes the principled inadequacy of Kant's pre-third-*Critique* theoretical philosophy for capturing beautiful things and organic beings in their own right.

At a metacritical level, this inadequacy reveals that the grounding relation between a priori determining principles and a posteriori determining judgments – a relation at the structural core of Kant's pre-third-*Critique* theoretical philosophy – cannot be a fruitful model to explain (à la Beck et al.) how we gain access to beauty

---

[41]  See Allison (2001, 174).     [42]  See also Zuckert (2007, 341–343).     [43]  See A 21n.
[44]  See UTP, 08:181.11–21.

and biology in a duly critical teleology governed by a transcendental principle of the reflecting power of judgment. Specifically, that model cannot capture how the a priori principle of reflection is present "in" (CJ, 5:288.23) reflecting judgments, leaving the relation either too loose,[45] or too tight,[46] or too unsystematic.[47] To claim that the principle of reflection "underlies and licenses" (Allison 2001, 174) those judgments *en façon déterminante* and, so, to consider them, at least in this regard, "comparable ... to objective empirical cognitive judgments" (Beck 1978, 169) upends Kant's signature innovations in the third *Critique* (see Sections 4.4.1–7) and, a fortiori, forfeits any hope of explaining the third *Critique* as a critique.

There is a set of innovative and unconventional ideas at the core of Kant's *Critique of the Power of Judgment*. This is not surprising. If Kant's attempt to explain how intellects like ours gain principled access to a world of beautiful things and biological beings did not supersede the transcendental-logical conventions of Kant's pre-third-*Critique* theoretical philosophy, it would not have been worth the trouble. Kant's ideas coalesce in the doctrine of the apriority of first-order reflecting judgments of purposiveness. Like the phenomena it is supposed to capture, however, the doctrine itself presents an enigma. Let us see if we can crack Kant's code.

### 2.2.4 Natura Facit Saltūs

Any solution to the exegetical problem Kant's doctrine of the apriority of first-order reflecting judgments of purposiveness poses must begin by taking seriously Kant's idea that, in an encounter with beautiful things and organized beings, our ordinary empirical-scientific explanations are not just accidentally or temporarily stumped but that these phenomena cannot – in principle – be captured within the spatiotemporal and categorial epistemic framework expounded in the *Critique of Pure Reason*.[48] That is to say, any solution must take seriously Kant's idea that, by the lights of ordinary empirical-scientific cognition, we encounter a form of absolute cognitive limit in these phenomena.[49]

It will be helpful to put the possibility of such a limit in a broader, systematic perspective. In the *Critique of Pure Reason*, Kant was deeply committed to – albeit notoriously unable to justify – an objective interpretation of reason's heuristic principle of the continuity of nature: "*natura non facit*

---

[45] This is manifest in interpretations according to which that a priori ground (a) concerns only the judgment type (not its tokens), (b) is unavailable (and may not be needed to begin with), and (c) must be sought elsewhere (e.g., in Kant's moral philosophy or rational theology).

[46] See note 42.

[47] The difficulties with explaining the a priori ground of aesthetic and teleological judgments compound the difficulties with explaining how it can be the same a priori ground in both cases.

[48] See CJ, 5:359.14–360,01; see also Section 5.2.     [49] See CJ, 5:285.22–24, 410.07–08.

*saltus*."[50] As a heuristic principle, "*natura non facit saltus*" is a maximalist yet open-ended principle, in keeping with its status as both principle of reason and research-guiding maxim. "Nature makes no leap" exhorts us *to seek*, in our cognition of the world, an unbroken continuity in the set of natural conditions. But Kant saw no way to justify the peculiar bindingness of this subjective and research-guiding maxim, except by grounding it in a philosophically weightier, objective counterpart. As an objective principle, "*natura non facit saltus*" not only exhorts us to seek an unbroken continuity in the set of natural conditions – it declares one. Now, a "leap," or a break in the continuity of natural conditions, would be a state or event in nature that in principle defies causal-scientific explanation. Accordingly, as an objective principle, "*natura non facit saltus*" declares that there are no parts of nature that are not – in principle – capable of being integrated into a continuous, hierarchical network of rational, scientific cognitions. In other words, it declares that there are no parts of nature that are not – in principle – cognizable, which is to say: it declares that, in nature, there are no absolute cognitive limits.

Not surprisingly, Kant was unable to find transcendental-philosophical warrant for such an expansive, dogmatically flavored principle.[51] As a result, he was not able to justify reason's merely heuristic maxim of nature's continuity either. Apparently chastened by this outcome, Kant, in 1790, changed tactics. In the third *Critique*, rather than seek to establish nature's maximal continuity as an objective principle of reason, Kant sought to establish a mere assumption of nature's minimal continuity as a principle of the reflecting power of judgment. Kant's characteristic third-*Critique* line of argument is that, once we have established, for the reflecting power of judgment, the transcendental necessity of an assumption of nature's minimal continuity, the faculty of reason "may go further" and assume, as a heuristic maxim, nature's much more thoroughgoing continuity; consonant with reason's own maximizing tendencies but without requiring additional transcendental warrant.

This general shift in strategy for justifying reason's heuristic principle of the continuity of nature – from a 1780s-style, reason-centered, maximalist justification to a 1790s-style, reflecting-judgment-centered, minimalist justification – has an important consequence that now takes center stage: it opens up the space in which aesthetic and biological phenomena can live. For the flip side of Kant's

---

[50] Kant does not use this (standard) Latin formulation, which comes to us from Leibniz. Kant instead renders the principle as: "'Nature . . . makes no leap; either in the sequence of its changes or in the juxtaposition of its forms'" (CJ, 5:182.20–22). For discussion of this and Kant's other cosmological principles, see Watkins (2019, 193–207).

[51] See Bennett (1974, 280), Horstmann (1989, 166), Guyer (1990, 28), Kemp-Smith (1992, 552), Grier (1997, 14–15).

abandonment of the commitment to a maximalist objective interpretation of nature's continuity – hence, the flip side of Kant's abandonment of the commitment to a principle of nature's in-principle cognizability – is that in principle *un*cognizable dimensions of nature are neither metaphysically impossible nor rationally impermissible. The idea of such dimensions is, to the contrary, the central premise of Kant's efforts to integrate the phenomena of beauty and biological organization into his critical philosophy in 1790.

If the third *Critique* had a motto, it would have to be "*natura facit saltūs*" – with beauty and biological organization (the phenomenal manifestations of) the leaps in question.

But if in-principle uncognizable aspects of the world have thus become a metaphysical possibility for Kant, such *saltūs* (if any) must nevertheless remain, ex hypothesi, cognitively – and, a fortiori, experientially – unavailable by the lights of Kant's account of human cognition in the *Critique of Pure Reason*. Accordingly, the transcendental-philosophical task Kant sets for himself in the *Critique of the Power of Judgment* is to explain how, given the third *Critique*'s expanded sense of our cognitive makeup, an encounter with absolute cognitive limits could nevertheless leave a mark in phenomenal consciousness. Without such an account, in-principle uncognizable aspects of the world would pass us by like ships in the dark. Accordingly, if an encounter with beauty and biological organization is an encounter with some form of absolute cognitive limit, then, in the absence of such an account, beauty and biological organization would remain inexplicable for critical philosophy.

As noted before, however, the third *Critique* is not post-critical. The principal philosophical constraints on Kant's account are that it (a) not run afoul of the prohibition Kant places on cognition of things in themselves in the first *Critique* and (b) be explicative of the cognitive phenomenology of our engagement with beauty and biological organization Kant presents in the two Analytics of the third *Critique*. Kant's twin theories of a priori reflecting (aesthetic) judgments of a "purposiveness without purpose" and of a priori reflecting (teleological) judgments of a "purposiveness with purpose" represent Kant's answer to the question what form the sought-for mark in phenomenal consciousness must take.

Kant's foundational idea – as dictated by the structure of his account – is that, when confronted with an in-principle cognitive limit (as in an encounter with beauty and biological organization), all there is for us to encounter is our own a priori cognitive posture in the form of the reflecting power of judgment's self-given and self-governing principle of nature's purposiveness, namely the reflecting power of judgment's a priori demand for an assumption of nature's inexistent conceptual order. Ordinarily, this principle operates at a subpersonal level, according to the cognitive role assigned to it by its transcendental deduction. That role is, roughly, to render as yet uncognized (namely unsynthesized) sensible material amenable to cognitive uptake by assuming it to be minimally cognizable (hence synthesizable). Why uncognized sensible material should stand in need of such transcendental-philosophical rendition – given everything that Kant had already said about the matter in the *Critique of Pure Reason* – hence, what Kant's justification for the new transcendental principle of nature's purposiveness might be, is the topic of Sections 4.3.2 and 4.4.1–2.

For present purposes, the thing to note is the cognitive phenomenology of the operation of this principle. The reflecting power of judgment's a priori demand for an assumption of nature's purposiveness (namely of nature's inexistent conceptual order and, a fortiori, cognizability and synthesizability) is directed, in the first place, at the reflecting power of judgment *itself*: the reflecting power of judgment alone can satisfy that demand by making the assumption so demanded. The demand is directed, in the second place, at the world: the world alone can satisfy the assumption so made, by proving to *be* synthesizable.

In the case of ordinary empirical cognition, both of these demands are met. The satisfaction of the first demand is, moreover, not only unremarkable, since it is transcendental-philosophically assured, but goes unremarked, since it is discharged in the formation of actual empirical cognition of the world. In the case of an encounter with an in-principle uncognizable aspect of the world, by contrast, the second of these demands ex hypothesi cannot be met. The satisfaction of the first demand is here still unremarkable, since it is still transcendental-philosophically assured. But it no longer goes unremarked. Since the assumption made is not absorbed in downstream determining judgments, it is left dangling like a question mark over the respective cognitive episode. Its entreaty unanswered, the reflecting power of judgments' a priori assumption of purposiveness here instead registers as an in-principle unfulfilled, empirically unsupported, and consequently quasi-auratic sense of the presence of conceptual order. Since this a priori assumption of purposiveness can, moreover, only come to self-conscious awareness in the context of otherwise fully spatiotemporally and conceptually determined self-conscious experience, it can only become cognitively manifest as a judgment of some *object* or other – albeit not prompted by any object's actual, observable features.

The resulting judgment of purposiveness is then (a) a *reflecting* judgment (because it is a manifestation of the reflecting power of judgment's self-given and self-governing assumption of nature's conceptual order), (b) a *logically singular* judgment (because that assumption is here manifest in the context of my cognition of an otherwise sensibly given, spatiotemporally individuated, and empirically determined object), (c) an a priori judgment (because the assumption so manifest is not a response to any of this or any other object's empirical features), (d) a *predicatively holistic* judgment (because, as an assumption of the object's origin in *its* concept, it extends to the object in its entirety), (e) a judgment accompanied by a *quasi-auratic awareness* of its object's artifactuality (because, thus manifest in a nondetermining, empirically ungrounded judgment, this predicative holism can only come to be phenomenally manifest as an ineffable cognitive sense that the object originated in its concept). This complex cognitive structure – an a priori reflecting judgment of purposiveness – is the fundamental vehicle for all other doctrines of Kant's aesthetics and philosophy of biology.

In terms of the aforementioned constraints on Kant's account, we can now see the following. First, because it is at bottom an awareness of our own form of judging, an a priori reflecting judgment of purposiveness is not a determinate cognition of a transcendent (nor, for that matter, of an immanent) object. Accordingly, it does not run afoul of Kant's prohibition against knowledge of things in themselves. Second, Kant holds that there are two general ways in which an a priori reflecting judgment of purposiveness can come to self-conscious awareness: as an a priori reflecting (aesthetic) judgment of a "purposiveness without purpose" or as an a priori reflecting (teleological) judgment of a "purposiveness with purpose." Accordingly, whether Kant's theory of a priori reflecting judgments of purposiveness captures the characteristic features of our engagement with beautiful things and organisms, which Kant presents in the respective Analytics of his aesthetics and teleology, depends on Kant's account of the effect, on these judgments, of the respective absence or presence of a putative "purpose." To purposes, in short, we must turn.

### 2.2.5 Purpose

If purposiveness, according to Kant's backward-looking, etiological definition of the term, is "the causality of a concept with respect to its object," then a "purpose" just is the object or product generated in instances of conceptual causality. To identify an object as a purpose in this sense thus involves a backward-looking, etiological characterization of the thing in terms of a causal and representational link to its concept as well. Along the causal dimension, judging an object to be a purpose highlights the presumed fact that *a* concept figured somewhere along the chain of causes that terminated in the object. Along the representational dimension, judging an object to be a purpose highlights the presumed fact that *its* concept figured somewhere along the chain of causes that terminated in the object.

Here, too, we must emphasize Kant's distinction between transcendental and empirical determinations. According to its transcendental determinations, considering an object to be a purpose concerns the metaphysical circumstance that, for it to be a product of conceptual causality at all, there must be a representational link, in addition to a causal link, connecting the object to a (namely its) concept. Empirical determinations concerning what that representational link may be, how we may know it, how faithfully it has been realized, etcetera, are, once again, irrelevant to that transcendental perspective.

We can begin to appreciate Kant's philosophical modus operandi in the *Critique of the Power of Judgment* by observing that attributing purposiveness in this transcendental sense to an object in an a priori reflecting judgment of purposiveness analytically entails considering the object to be a purpose in just that transcendental sense. If I posit the presence of a representational link between an object and its putative conceptual cause, I eo ipso consider the object in question to be a purpose in the transcendental sense. Any a priori reflecting judgment that attributes purposiveness in the transcendental sense to an object is therefore an a priori reflecting judgment that considers the object a purpose in just that sense. Denying that the object is a purpose in the transcendental sense, even as I attribute purposiveness in just that sense to it, would, accordingly, be a contradiction in terms. Highlighting that the object is a purpose in the transcendental sense, just as I attribute purposiveness in that sense to it, would, accordingly, be redundant. Why, then, does Kant nevertheless do just that: deny that the object is a purpose, when he characterizes a priori reflecting judgments in his aesthetics as addressing a "purposiveness … without purpose" (CJ, 5:220.22–23); highlight that the object is a purpose, when he characterizes a priori reflecting judgments in his teleology as addressing a purposiveness with purpose (see CJ, 5:359.14–16)? The answer is that, rather than contradict himself or indulge in empty pronouncements, Kant here lets transcendental and empirical dimensions of attributions of purposiveness interact with each other. That is the philosophical engine that propels Kant's critical teleology in the *Critique of the Power of Judgment*.

### 2.2.6 *Purposiveness* without *Purpose*, *Purposiveness* with *Purpose*

To say, as Kant does in his aesthetics, that there can be an a priori judgment that attributes purposiveness to an object but that nevertheless does not consider the object to be a purpose is to envision a scenario in which the transcendental and empirical determinations of an object's being a purpose come apart.[52] It is to say that we can have a sense of the presence of the representational dimension in a purported instance of conceptual causality without a corresponding grasp of the content of the normative constraint that representational dimension imposes or of the degree of its satisfaction, etcetera.

---

[52] See CJ, 5:220.22–23.

To get comfortable with the idea, we may imagine, as does Kant, the case of sophisticated ancient or alien tools or of other highly unusual artifacts.[53] We know them to be products of intelligent agency but, beyond that, we have no idea what they may be. This, to be sure, is a case of a posteriori, determining judgments of purposiveness. By contrast, Kant's aesthetic scenario concerns a priori reflecting judgments of purposiveness, in which our inability to determine the content of the object's purported conceptual cause is not due to an accident of situation or a failure of imagination but reflective of an in-principle cognitive limit. While being the result of an encounter with an in-principle cognitive limit is the defining characteristic of all a priori reflecting judgments, that characteristic is particularly pronounced in the aesthetic case. Here, we can not only not know why a specific object warrants dispositive aesthetic appraisal, we cannot even arrive at a determinative judgment of what *kind* of object does so either. If we could, ours would no longer be an aesthetic appraisal. In the absence of determining warrant for the purposiveness my judgment attributes to the thing, that judgment is, accordingly, an a priori reflecting judgment of a (transcendental) purposiveness without (empirical) purpose. I may, of course, have a general conception of what kind of thing I tend to find beautiful (that's why I keep going back to the opera). But that general conception is neither itself a judgment of taste nor can it provide the ground for one. Any liking that can be stated in terms of or derived from an object's empirical properties must fail to be a judgment of taste in Kant's sense.

A reflecting aesthetic judgment, accordingly, is an a priori judgment marked by (a) the quasi-auratic sense that an otherwise perceptually given and fully conceptually determined object, in addition, exhibits a causal as well as a representational link to a putative causally efficacious concept – its concept; (b) an in-principle cognitive limit barring any determinate grasp of what that putative concept might be; (c) an in-principle absence, even, of inferentially related post hoc generalizations about this, lest the judgment cease to be aesthetic altogether.

According to Kant's aesthetics, such nonempirical, holistic attributions of purposiveness are, moreover, made with respect to empirically nonpurposive, natural objects as well as with respect to empirically purposive, artifactual objects. In either case, these attributions carry in their phenomenal wake delicate theoretical dissonances (respectively, the felt presence of a conceptual cause in a natural object that patently does *not* have one and the felt absence of a purpose in an artifactual object that patently *does* have one) and correlated cognitive and affective reverberations that Kant analyzes – at length – as characteristic of our

---

[53] See CJ, 5:236n.

fully formed engagement with natural and artistic beauty and as part of any full-fledged reflecting judgment of taste.

The teleological case runs essentially parallel to the aesthetic scenario, with one crucial difference. We here do command determinative post hoc generalizations of just what kind of thing warrants nonempirical attributions of an origin in conceptual causality – namely biological organisms.[54] More to the point, we muster a wealth of biological knowledge that helps us flesh out in great detail what parts, properties, and processes of organisms we so appraise – even as the purposiveness in question itself "cannot be perceived" (CJ, 5:189.22). Thus equipped with compensatory insight into the kind of thing to which our a priori reflecting judgments attribute an origin in concepts, those judgments, accordingly, diagnose a (transcendental) purposiveness with (empirical) purpose. Because of the presence of recurrent observable features (parts, properties, and processes) we so appraise, the cognitive phenomenology of these attributions differs markedly from that of their aesthetic counterparts.[55] This is best seen by considering the issue of the teleological loop.

### 2.2.7 The Teleological Loop

In the case of the absence of a post hoc, compensatory grasp of the concept in which my a priori reflecting judgment of purposiveness locates a given object's origin, I can give no teleological appraisal of that object either. Here, the loop-generating idea that the *causa formalis* (what-it-is) supplies the *causa finalis* (that-for-the-sake-of-which) is moot. A teleological loop still attends, but only in an attenuated, theoretical sense. Ex hypothesi devoid of articulable content, it is not only not logically worrisome but also not heuristically fruitful. Neither vertiginous nor virtuous it is, instead, just vacuous. Rather than being distracted by a teleological loop, my mind here struggles with the empirically unsupported, quasi-auratic sense of surplus conceptual order that my a priori reflecting attribution of purposiveness to the object entails. This "occasions much thinking, though without it being possible for any determinate thought, i.e., concept, to be adequate to it" (CJ, 5:314.02–04). As a result, it generates the distinctive phenomenology of our engagement with natural and artistic beauty

---

[54] See CJ, 5:194.12–15.

[55] The beauty of organisms (see CJ, 5:215.21, 299.09–10) represents a special case. Beautiful organisms are supersensibly overdetermined. They are, in the first place, objects of an a priori reflecting judgment of a (transcendental) purposiveness *with* (empirical) purpose and, *additionally*, of an a priori reflecting judgment of a (transcendental) purposiveness *without* (empirical) purpose. These characterizations need not be inconsistent. Much like "the supersensible substratum of appearances" (CJ, 5:341.01) can ground multiple *determinations* of those appearances, it can also sustain more than one *reflection* (see Section 5.4.4).

that Kant discusses in the "Analytic of the Critique of the Aesthetic Power of Judgment" (CJ, 5:302.02).

By contrast, in the case of the presence of a post hoc, compensatory grasp of the concept in which my a priori reflecting judgment of purposiveness locates a given object's origin, that grasp entails a sense also of its *causa finalis* since, as Aristotle taught, empirically, the two "are one" (Aristotle 1985, 30). We here accordingly have an extraneous grasp of the empirical determinations of the thing as a purpose not only in Kant's sense of the term (as "product of conceptual causality") but also in the traditional sense of the term (as "end-state" or "*telos*"). By identifying the "what-it-is" (e.g., that the "organ in question manages to pump blood"; Neander and Schulte, 1991, 180) with the "that-for-the-sake-of-which" (namely that "that is what it is supposed to do"; 180), we are characterizing the object's coming-into-being in standard teleological fashion in terms of its effect. Or, as Kant now puts it, we judge the thing as a "natural purpose" (CJ, 5:370.31).

It is of greatest importance for Kant's philosophy of biology that this post hoc grasp of the kind of thing that merits a priori reflecting attributions of an origin in concepts picks out objects of a reliably similar kind: organisms and their parts and processes. But note, first, that this does not affect the logical singularity of those a priori reflecting attributions of purposiveness, no more than a beautiful object's empirical determinations affect the singularity of my judgment of taste. The difference is that my a priori reflecting attribution of purposiveness here aligns with empirical determinations that instantiate patterns that make a science of those objects possible. Note, second, that however unknowable the source of that alignment may ex hypothesi be, finding the objects of that science marked by the ensuing contentful teleological loop accordingly does not appear arbitrary. Kant instead treats their functional appraisal as symptomatic of their inner (if hidden) nature and recommends we use this teleology as a heuristic guide in our empirical research into those objects and beyond (see Section 5.5).

## 2.3 Empirical Teleology?

There is a straightforward objection to my account of Kant's theory of teleological judgments as a theory of a priori reflecting judgments of a "purposiveness with purpose." We do not have to turn to causal-role theories in the contemporary philosophy of biology to learn that there are empirical, systems-theoretic properties that justify our functional appraisal of organisms and their parts and processes. Kant himself, in the Analytic of the Teleological Power of Judgment, proposes an analysis of natural purposiveness in terms of just such properties. Specifically, he points to distinctive reciprocal causal interactions among an organism's parts and processes as well as to a related unique form of part–whole interdependence as the ground for our treatment of organisms as natural *telē*.[56] It appears, then, that these empirical features – rather than mysterious uncognizable aspects of the world (nature's "*saltūs*") – underwrite teleological judgments of organic beings for Kant.

Interpreting the teleological Analytic in this manner, while plausible on the surface, is based on a misunderstanding of the argument structure of the second part of the third *Critique* in general and of the teleological Analytic in particular. Just as Kant's teleological Dialectic is an unusual Dialectic (because it arises on *non*dogmatic, critical grounds and so poses a threat to critical philosophy itself; see Section 3.1), Kant's teleological Analytic, similarly, does not follow the standard playbook of Kantian Analytics.[57] According to that playbook, a transcendental analytic provides a conceptual analysis and a transcendental justification of some synthetic a priori principle or other. By that standard, Kant's teleological Analytic not only disappoints but must be deemed positively subversive. For the point of Kant's teleological Analytic is to show that the confident promises of conceptual analyses of biological teleology vastly exceed what they can deliver.

The teleological Analytic does begin with an initially promising account that identifies biological teleology with the reciprocal causal processes involved in reproduction, self-maintenance, and growth,[58] following standard views at the time.[59] But an analysis of the teleological nature of these processes soon dissolves as Kant shows that, to the extent that they can be explained, there is nothing distinctively teleological about them and, to the extent that they are teleological, they cannot be explained.[60]

Empirically, the teleological dimension of organized beings in nature remains a wholly "inscrutable property" (CJ, 5:374.33–34) or a property "not thinkable and explicable" (CJ, 5:375.16) for intellects like ours. First, we cannot "think and explain" it through an analogy with "any physical, i.e., natural capacity that is known to us" (CJ, 5:375.13) since the physical form of causality known to us is mechanistic and so nonteleological. Second, we cannot "think and explain" it through an analogy with teleological forms of causality since the one known to us would make it "an accurately tailored analogy with human art" (CJ, 5:375.15–16) and, so, with a form of causality that is nonnatural. Kant concludes that "the organization of nature is therefore not analogous with any causality that we know" (CJ, 5:375.05–07). To be sure, this does not change the phenomenological fact from which the Critique of the

---

[56] See CJ, 5:370.36–37; 5:373.26–34.    [57] See Teufel (2023, 261).
[58] See CJ, 5:371.07–372.11.    [59] See McLaughlin (2001, 177–178).
[60] See CJ, 5:374.33–375.07.

Teleological Power of Judgment proceeds that "organized beings ... must nevertheless be thought of as possible only as its [N.B.: nature's] purposes" (CJ, 5:375.27–28). But while the teleological Analytic further characterizes that peculiar phenomenon, it does not – and it offers the reasons why it cannot – provide an analysis let alone a transcendental justification of the concept of "natural purpose" under investigation, a first among Kantian Analytics.

To think that the teleological Analytic is therefore a failure would, however, be to adopt too narrow a perspective. Kant's teleological Analytic is the *locus classicus* of a *reductio ad absurdum* of the hopeful idea, popular to this day, that we can somehow cash in our sense of the teleology of organic beings in terms of a systems-theoretic understanding of their causal properties. Kant's strategic aim in showing the futility of such conceptual analyses is to shift the burden of proof to the teleological Dialectic and the transcendental-philosophical justification of a priori reflecting judgments of purposiveness he attempts there (see Sections 3–5).

## 2.4 Essential Aesthetics?

There is another straightforward objection to an account that identifies Kant's critical teleology with the *Critique of the Power of Judgment* at large (and so does not limit Kant's critical teleology to Kant's philosophy of biology in the Critique of the Teleological Power of Judgment). Given Kant's subdivision of the book, Kant's aesthetics and Kant's philosophy of biology would, on the present hypothesis, appear to be of roughly equal importance to Kant's critical teleology in the *Critique of the Power of Judgment*. But Kant rather pointedly disagrees, declaring only his aesthetics and *not* his philosophy of biology "essential" (CJ, 5:193.25) to a critique of judgment. But if Kant's critique of judgment is essentially an aesthetics and not a philosophy of biology, then, if Kant's critique of judgment and Kant's critical teleology were effectively the same thing, Kant's critical philosophy of biology would not be essential to Kant's critical teleology. That would be absurd. It appears that an account that limits Kant's critical teleology to Kant's philosophy of biology and does not identify it with Kant's critique of judgment at large accords better with Kant's views.

The dynamic here is fascinating because Kant's aesthetics is both more central *and* less central to Kant's critical teleology than Kant's philosophy of biology. Because of the absence of a post hoc, compensatory grasp of the concept in which a priori reflecting aesthetic judgments of purposiveness locate their object's origin, they are the purest expression, in phenomenal consciousness, of the ordinarily subpersonal role of the transcendental principle of nature's purposiveness. They are singular judgments of empirically given objects "according to a [N.B.: transcendental] rule but not according to [N.B.: empirical] concepts" (CJ, 5:194.23). They reveal what, in essence, a priori reflection on discrete objects governed by a transcendental principle of purposiveness amounts to. But the absence of a purpose here not only means that such judgments do not generate a fruitful teleological loop; it means that they exist in a near-frictionless cognitive realm of their own, integrated with ordinary cognitive processes only by means of an allegedly seamless and enjoyable "free play" (CJ, 5:217.22) rather than by hard-won logical subordination. Their purity thus comes at a price. Exactly how we are to imagine the interaction between free and bound – between playful and more effortful – forms of judging raises a host of difficulties unique to Kant's aesthetics. But no matter how we address these perplexities, a priori reflecting aesthetic judgments stand apart from ordinary cognition and, as a result, put relatively little pressure on the rest of Kant's critical epistemology. Central as they may be to a critique of judgment, they do not tell us much about the relation between their a priori principle and, most importantly, the pure concepts of the understanding in the *Critique of Pure Reason*.

That part of the story is told in Kant's critical philosophy of biology. This is because a priori reflecting teleological judgments function more like ordinary theoretical judgments than do a priori reflecting aesthetic judgments. Because of their characteristic admixture of a post hoc, compensatory grasp of the concept in which my judgment locates the object's origin, they are not nearly as revealing of the pure "essence" of a priori reflection on the world as their aesthetic counterparts. By the same token, any account of a priori reflecting judgments of a purposiveness with purpose requires an explanation of how the same natural properties and processes can be appraised teleologically and mechanistically at the same time.

In the context of Kant's critical teleology, the relative priority of Kant's aesthetics over Kant's philosophy of biology is, accordingly, a matter of approach. If our guiding research interest in Kant's critical teleology concerns what unadulterated a priori reflection on the world amounts to, then Kant's aesthetics is the natural place to start. If, however, our guiding research interest in Kant's critical teleology concerns the tension between a priori reflection and ordinary empirical ways of knowing, then Kant's philosophy of biology must be the focus.

The latter is the focus here, for two related reasons. First, the tension, in Kant's philosophy of biology, between a priori reflection and ordinary empirical ways of knowing, relates Kant's critical teleology to the concerns of traditional teleology. Kant is right to consider his philosophy of biology and not his aesthetics a "teleology" (CJ, 5:361.01) in the traditional, end-involving sense because it alone deals with articulable *telē*, the noted tension, and a consequent pronounced and fruitful teleological loop.

Second, the tension between a priori reflection and ordinary empirical ways of knowing requires Kant to address the reflecting power of judgment in its dialectical complications in the teleological antinomy at the heart of the teleological Dialectic.[61] The resolution of this antinomy provides the sought-for transcendental-philosophical justification of a priori reflecting judgments of purposiveness (both with and without purpose). Once again, we find that the burden of proof of Kant's argument lies with the teleological Dialectic. To the Dialectic we must, accordingly, turn.

## 3 Purposiveness as Transcendental Principle

### 3.1 Introduction: Outside the Box

When approaching the "Dialectic of the Teleological Power of Judgment" (CJ, 5:385.02) we find almost immediately that not all matters crucially important to it are explicitly addressed in it. In particular, the resolution of the teleological antinomy at the heart of the Dialectic requires us to understand a range of broader theoretical issues that seem to have little immediate bearing on biological teleology. The reason for this is that, even as the antinomy becomes a live issue only in the context of competing forms of judgment of organized beings in nature, it is, at bottom, a clash between the powers of reflection and determination themselves. No mere sideshow in the critical universe, Kant presents it as a full-blown "Antinomy of the Power of Judgment" (CJ, 5:385.04). Now, both powers – the reflecting power of judgment and the determining power of judgment, or the understanding[62] – have their own transcendental-philosophical justification[63] within Kant's critical philosophy. Accordingly, the conflict between them ex hypothesi arises on nondogmatic,

---

[61] The Critique of the Aesthetic Power of Judgment of course also contains a Dialectic. But its central dialectical conflict is not a battle between the powers of reflection and determination themselves that arises from the *presence* of a purpose in a priori reflecting teleological judgments of purposiveness. It is instead a more familiar "antinomy of reason" (CJ, 5:345.14–15), arising from the *absence* of a purpose in a priori reflecting aesthetic judgments.

[62] See A 69/B 94.

[63] The main instances of transcendental principles in the *Critique of Pure Reason* are a priori constitutive principles of the understanding. But Kant's conception of the nature of transcendental cognition does not limit that cognition to constitutive principles. Kant says, "I call all cognition *transcendental* that is occupied not so much with objects but rather with our mode of cognition of objects in general, insofar as this [N.B.: mode of cognition] is to be possible a priori" (A 11–12/B 25, Kant's emphasis). Transcendental cognition, then, is a priori cognition of a priori cognition, or a priori metacognition. Regulative transcendental principles, occupied with a priori object-determination by governing it in nonconstitutive but nevertheless a priori and necessary ways are fully within the purview of such metacognition. See Teufel (2017, 117).

duly critical grounds. This makes the teleological antinomy unusual among Kantian antinomies. Its resolution does not call for a critical reinterpretation of competing dogmatic positions but for a metacritical integration of competing critical positions.[64] As a consequence, the teleological antinomy has a different strategic role and arguably higher philosophical stakes than other Kantian antinomies. Kant is on defense. Rather than establish critical philosophy as a powerful tool to vanquish rational and empirical dogmatisms, the resolution of the teleological antinomy has the less glamorous and rather more existential task of showing that critical philosophy itself is free from contradiction. Instead of demonstrating critical prowess, Kant must avert critical chaos (one of three types of cognitive chaos – empirical, transcendental, and critical – I discuss in Sections 4 and 5). If the sought-for metacritical integration were unavailable – if the conflict between reflection and determination were not merely the "natural and unavoidable" (CJ, 5:340.27–28) appearance of a contradiction but the genuine article – then a critical edifice that contains both a *Critique of the Power of Judgment* (centered around the reflecting power of judgment) and a *Critique of Pure Reason* (centered around the capacity to make determining judgments) would, accordingly, be a self-contradictory edifice.

The range of theoretical issues we need to understand in order to see how Kant resolves the Antinomy of the Power of Judgment can be fruitfully organized in terms of the earlier image of the third *Critique* as a black box. We cannot understand Kant's critical teleology and, specifically, how the a priori reflecting judgments of natural purposes that come "out of" the box can be consistent with the rest of Kant's critical epistemology (see Section 5.5), unless we understand what goes on "inside" the box – specifically, how a priori reflecting judgments of a purposiveness with (and without) purpose are grounded in the transcendental principle of the reflecting power of judgment (see Section 5.4). And we cannot understand the nature of this grounding, unless we understand the nature of the principle of the reflecting power of judgment that goes "into" the box – specifically, its transcendental justification, claim, cognitive role, structure, and normative status (see Section 4.4). Finally, we cannot understand what goes into the box, unless we understand what must remain "outside" it and why – specifically, why Kant's first two attempts at a transcendental deduction of the principle of nature's purposiveness fail (see Section 3.2).

## 3.2 False Start(s)

Kant offers three separate attempts at a transcendental justification of the principle that eventually becomes the transcendental principle of the reflecting power of judgment. The first attempt seeks to justify a principle of nature's

---

[64] See Teufel (2023, 261).

"systematic unity" (A647–648/B 675–676) in the Appendix to the Dialectic of the *Critique of Pure Reason* (see Section 3.2.1). The second attempt is Kant's official but oddly inconclusive "deduction" (CJ, 5:184.22) of the mature "Principle of the Formal Purposiveness of Nature" (CJ, 5:181.13) in §V of the Introduction of the *Critique of the Power of Judgment* (see Sections 3.2.2–3). The third attempt is a renewed stab at that same deduction in the justly famous §§76–77 of the teleological Dialectic, apparently prompted by the shortcomings of the earlier deduction as well as by the urgent need for a transcendental-philosophical resolution of the teleological antinomy. This third attempt is successful and yields the argument that allows Kant to resolve the antinomy, integrate reflection and determination, and save critical philosophy itself from internal contradiction (see Sections 4 and 5).

### 3.2.1 Nature's Systematic Unity (Appendix to the Dialectic)

Kant's first attempt, in the Appendix to the Dialectic of the *Critique of Pure Reason*, to secure transcendental status for the principle that will eventually become the transcendental principle of the purposiveness of nature in the *Critique of the Power of Judgment* neither mentions a reflecting power of judgment (which Kant had not identified yet) nor relates the principle to philosophical teleology. The connection between Kant's argument in the first *Critique* and his later arguments in the third *Critique* is that all concern a principle of natural order: nature's "systematic unity" in the first *Critique*, nature's "purposiveness" in the third *Critique*.

Kant's argument for the apriority and necessity of a synthetic principle of natural order in the first *Critique* is marked by four main characteristics. First, Kant construes the principle as an *objective* principle or a principle that captures a fundamental feature of reality: *nature*'s underlying systematic unity or "systematic unity, *as pertaining to the object itself*" (A 650/B 678, my emphasis). Second, Kant construes this principle as a principle of reason or a principle that, despite this objective import, is not constitutive of the objects of outer sense but instead presents an idea of totality – the idea of nature's *maximal* systematic unity. Third, Kant construes this principle as, in fact, composed of three distinct principles – the principles of nature's "*manifoldness, affinity* and *unity*" (A 662/ B 690; Kant's emphasis). Fourth, Kant's argument for the transcendental status of these objective, rational principles of nature's maximal systematic unity is premised on the alleged impossibility – were nature not maximally unified – to justify a corresponding set of merely heuristic maxims of systematic unity (the maxims of nature's *specificity, continuity,* and *homogeneity*) that are "subjectively and logically necessary, as method" (A 648/B 676).

Kant takes the peculiar form of methodological bindingness ("subjective and logical" necessity) of the latter, merely heuristic maxims of nature's systematic unity for granted. He does so, presumably on the pragmatic ground that much of empirical science appears to be subject to it (one need only consider the centuries-long drive toward grand unifications in physics to appreciate the point). But the presumed fact of this bindingness then serves as the minor premise in an argument whose major premise asserts that such bindingness could not possibly be justified, were heuristic maxims not grounded in a corresponding set of transcendental and objective principles of rational unity: "In fact it cannot even be seen how there could be a *logical principle* of rational unity among rules unless a *transcendental principle* is presupposed, through which such a systematic unity, *as pertaining to the object itself*, is assumed a priori as necessary" (A 650–1/B 678–9; my emphases).

Intuitively this makes sense. What would be the point of – how could we justify – promoting, say, parsimony in theory construction if such parsimony did not track a deeper truth about the world? Still, this attempt at a deduction of the transcendental status of an objective principle of nature's maximal systematic unity fails. If the necessity of research-guiding maxims were merely pragmatic (if it were the result of a happy coincidence), then no additional transcendental-philosophical warrant would be needed to support it. Conversely, if the necessity of research-guiding maxims were more than merely pragmatic because it is backed by a transcendental and objective principle of nature's maximal systematic unity, then it could not, on pain of circularity, serve as a premise in the argument for that principle. Only if Kant provided an independent argument for the more-than-merely pragmatic necessity of heuristic maxims of nature's systematic unity could that "subjective and logical" necessity serve in a non-question-begging argument for the transcendental status of an objective principle of nature's maximal systematic unity. Kant does not provide such an independent argument. In the absence of an independent argument for the more-than-merely pragmatic "subjective and logical" necessity of heuristic maxims of nature's systematic unity, the methodological necessity of these maxims accordingly remains unsupported. Kant's argument for the transcendental status of an objective principle of nature's maximal systematic unity premised on that methodological necessity is then either uncalled for (if the maxims were merely pragmatic, after all) or unfounded (since a non-circular interpretation is unavailable).

By rights, the argument for the transcendental status of an objective principle of nature's maximal systematic unity should have been the structural and dramatic high point of the *Critique of Pure Reason*. The argument was to establish this principle as the foremost example of the transcendental-philosophically legitimate or "good and *immanent*" (A 643/B 671; Kant's emphasis) use of ideas of pure theoretical reason. This was supposed to contrast with the illegitimate and "*transcendent*" (A 643/B 671; Kant's emphasis) use of ideas of pure reason Kant had discussed in the earlier, properly dialectical part of the Dialectic.

In the end, however, Kant is forced to admit that objective principles of nature's maximal systematic unity merely "*seem to be* transcendental" (A 663/B 691; my emphasis). This may be all we can expect from a text that belongs to a division of transcendental logic that Kant considers a "logic of illusion" (A 293/B 249).[65] It certainly is an appearance that is not fortified into a reality by Kant's comment that these principles are of an "objective but indeterminate validity" (A 663/B 691).

Kant is aware of the weakness of his argument (this may be why he tucked it into a mere "Appendix"). His increasingly urgent claims that, moreover, without a transcendental justification of the principle of nature's maximal systematic unity, "no coherent use of the understanding" (A 651/B 679) itself – or even "no experience" (A 654/B 682) at all – would be possible, do little more than express the sense that a transcendental principle must be lurking in the vicinity but nothing to establish what that principle might be or how it may be supported.

Despite this anticlimactic outcome, Kant does not part with his ambition to find transcendental grounds for a principle of nature's systematic unity. But he does part – and thoroughly – with the approach he pursued in the Appendix to the Dialectic of the *Critique of Pure Reason*.

### 3.2.2 The Necessity of Empirical Laws

When Kant revisits the matter in the Introduction of the *Critique of the Power of Judgment*, he changes his argument in its entirety – along each of the four dimensions mentioned (despite outwardly promoting an air of doctrinal continuity).

First, Kant's new principle of nature's systematic unity, "the principle of the formal purposiveness of nature" (CJ, 5:181.13) is now no longer an objective principle but "a subjective principle (a maxim)" (CJ, 5:184.15–16). That is to say, it is not a factive principle that purports to capture *nature* but a regulative principle that captures how we must *judge* nature. In the Appendix to the Dialectic of the first *Critique*, Kant considered only the heuristic maxims of nature's systematic unity regulative. Since they were merely heuristic, they were not candidates for transcendental status. In the third *Critique*, Kant finally distinguishes regulativity (or subjectivity in the sense of "judgment-governance") from heuristicity (or subjectivity in the sense of "subjective necessity"). This opens up the conceptual

---

[65]  See Grier (1997, 14–15).

space in which a regulative (judgment-governing) but non-heuristic (not merely subjectively necessary) maxim like the principle of nature's purposiveness can, moreover, be a transcendental principle.

Second, this transcendental yet regulative principle of nature's systematic unity is now no longer an expansive principle of reason but a principle of the more modest reflecting power of judgment. That is to say, it does not promote a speculative idea of nature's maximal unity but consists in a reflecting demand that we must judge nature as exhibiting at least a minimum of unifiability.

Third, while an evolving set of merely heuristic, research-guiding maxims continues to be associated with this transcendental principle (the "pronouncements of metaphysical wisdom"; CJ, 5:182.16–17),[66] the transcendental principle itself is now uniform – a single principle and not a set of three.

Fourth, and most important for our purposes here (since this is the part that remains in flux over the course of the third *Critique*), the argument for the transcendental status of this regulative, reflecting, and uniform principle is now no longer tied to these heuristic maxims. Instead, the argument for the transcendental status of the principle of nature's systematic unity does, at least in Kant's initial presentation, hinge on an alleged impossibility – were there no such principle – to justify the necessity of empirical causal laws of nature.

Prima facie, the latter development is a sign of progress. By tying the transcendental deduction of the principle of nature's purposiveness to what Kant in the "The Postulates of Empirical Thinking in General" (A 218/B 265) in the *Critique of Pure Reason* calls the "material necessity in existence" (A 226/B 279) of empirical laws of nature, the minor premise of Kant's deduction now stands on firmer ground because it has a measure of the independent transcendental-philosophical support its counterpart in the Appendix to the Dialectic lacked.

According to Kant's view in the Postulates, we must regard empirical laws of nature as necessary because only sequences of events that stand in accordance with necessary causal laws can be considered objective. And considering sequences of events as objective is of pivotal importance for Kant's critical epistemology: it alone allows us to fix the distinction between inner and outer representations, to first establish a determinate temporal order for our inner representations, and, in this way, to first account for fully self-conscious experience of the world around us and of ourselves in it.

---

[66] Specifically, a set of pre-deduction "pronouncements" (CJ, 5:182.16) and a set of post-deduction "propositions" (CJ, 5:185.05).

Now, despite this importance, Kant's first-Critique response to Hume's famous skeptical challenge – concerning the necessity of causal relations – seeks to establish only the necessity of the transcendental causal law ("every event has a cause"). This is surprising, given the centrality of the problem of the necessity of empirical causal sequences both to Hume's challenge and Kant's response to it. But Kant's approach is deliberate. Kant does not offer an additional argument for the necessity of empirical causal laws of nature in the *Critique of Pure Reason* because he does not consider that necessity to present a separate problem: " From this it follows that the criterion of necessity [N.B.: for successive states of substance in accordance with empirical laws of causality] lies *solely* in the law of possible experience that everything that happens is determined a priori through its cause in appearance." (A227/B289; my emphasis). Kant's reasoning appears to be that transcendental philosophy is not in the business of telling us *what* the empirical laws of nature are but that it does guarantee *that* empirical laws of nature, whatever they may be, are necessary. While it falls to natural science to work out, over the long haul, what the laws are, the epistemic aposteriority of those laws accordingly does not entail their contingency.

In the *Critique of the Power of Judgment*, this line of argument comes under attack because Kant now realizes that it presumes, without justification, that the empirical causal laws that natural science will eventually arrive at are going to be, if you will, *friendly* to each other. Unfriendly laws would threaten to undercut each others' transcendental-philosophically assured claim to necessity and, a fortiori, the critical epistemology that rides on that assurance. This places the necessity of empirical causal laws in urgent need of *additional* transcendental-philosophical support. In the transcendental deduction of the principle of nature's purposiveness in the Introduction of the third *Critique*, Kant seems intent to provide it.

Kant begins by noting that, contrary to his view in the Postulates, the necessity of empirical causal laws cannot be grounded "solely" in the transcendental causal law:

> Now, however, the objects of empirical cognition are still determined or, as far as one can judge a priori, determinable in a variety of ways, apart from that formal time-determination [N.B.: the transcendental principle of causality], that specifically distinct natures, besides what they have in common as belonging to nature in general, *can still be causes in infinitely manifold ways*; and each of these ways must (in accordance with the concept of a cause in general) have its rule, which is a law, and hence is accompanied by necessity, although given the constitution and the limits of our faculties of cognition we have no insight at all into this necessity. (CJ, 5:183.14–22; my emphasis)

The difficulty here is not simply that empirical causal laws of nature cannot be logically derived from the transcendental causal law (if they could be so derived, their claim to necessity would be unproblematic but it would come at the expense of their claim to being empirical).[67] Kant's thinking, rather, appears to be that in the absence of deductive entailment between the transcendental causal law and empirical causal laws, the transcendental causal law is compatible with any number of different empirical causal orders. The trouble is that, "as far as one can judge a priori," there is nothing to rule out that these compossible ("still determinable") empirical causal orders may, moreover, be co-actual or true of the same "specifically distinct natures" *at the same time.*

However exactly we may want to imagine a world of such wildly unruly ("infinitely manifold") causal relations – and the scenario is arguably only a way station on the road to Kant's actual concern (see Section 4.2) – initially it does not seem all that troubling. The possibility of multiple co-actual causal orders is an assertively theoretical threat that can, accordingly, be balanced by a posteriori considerations concerning the facts on the ground. The scenario should then not be terribly distressing to us since, thankfully, we do not inhabit such a causally disorderly world.

Initially, the scenario might also not appear to be terribly distressing to the critical philosopher. While our own (apparently) good causal fortune cannot be credited to transcendental philosophy, the Postulates' assurance of the necessity of empirical causal laws not only appears to continue to hold for our own world but it would even appear to hold for causally less fortunate realms. A world in which "specifically distinct natures" *were* causes in an infinite variety of ways would simply be a world exhibiting an infinite variety of duly categorially supported claims to necessity for each of those ways of being a cause. What, then, appears to be the problem?

The crucial (if unstated) premise in Kant's conception of the difficulty is that if we cannot rule out the possibility of an infinity of co-actual causal orders, then, "as far as we can judge a priori," we cannot rule out the possibility of co-actual causal orders that are in conflict with one another either. But then – by the Postulates' continued assurance – we cannot rule out the possibility of co-actual and conflicting claims to necessity. Now, any two conflicting claims to necessity must, qua claims to necessity, be contradictorily opposed to each other. And no two contradictorily opposed claims can both be true, or statements of law, or necessary together. Fully disposed to license illegitimate claims to necessity – and a fortiori unable to secure the unifiability of experience – the Postulates' gratuitous assurance of the necessity of empirical causal laws thus comes to transcendental-philosophical naught, not

---

[67] See Messina (2017, 133).

because of an inconsistency at the transcendental level but because of the possibility of disorder on the ground. As Kant puts the point, in such a world, "no thoroughgoing interconnection of empirical cognitions into a whole of experience would take place" (CJ, 5:183.30–31).

The lesson readily transfers to causally less disjointed realms. Here the transcendental causal law would be similarly incapable of ruling out – and would instead sanction – errant contradictory claims to empirical causal necessity. Indeed, for any given empirical causal law of whose necessity the transcendental law of causality assures us, it would assure us also of the necessity of its contradictory opposite, were the world in question to support it. And *that* is true, even if the world in question were our own. The Postulates' assurance of the necessity of empirical causal laws of nature is, accordingly, transcendental-philosophically hopeless, so long as the possibility of disorder at the empirical level – whether rampant or errant – cannot be ruled out on a priori grounds. Pace Kant's claim in the Postulates, "the law of possible experience that everything that happens is determined *a priori* through its cause in appearance" A227/B289) therefore *cannot* serve as the "sole" criterion of the necessity of successive states of substance in accordance with empirical causal laws.

### 3.2.3 The Lawfulness of the Contingent

With the pivotal matter of the necessity of empirical causal laws of nature thus as yet unresolved in critical philosophy – and with Kant's vaunted answer to Hume's causal skepticism accordingly precariously in the balance – Kant seeks relief in his new reflecting power of judgment:

> The power of judgment must thus assume it as an *a priori* principle for its own use that what is contingent for human insight in the particular (empirical) laws of nature nevertheless contains a lawful unity, not fathomable by us but still thinkable, in the combination of its manifold into one experience possible in itself. (CJ, 5:183.34–184.02)[68]

Consistent with his etiological conception of purposiveness, Kant considers this a priori assumption of lawful unity on the model of conceptual in-existence as "a principle of purposiveness" (CJ, 5:184.08–09), since the "lawfulness of the contingent is called purposiveness" (CJ, 5:404.27–28).

Kant's idea appears to be that an a priori assumption of conceptual order in what we "at the same time [cognize] as contingent in itself" (CJ, 5:184.04–05) offers just the assurance of lawful unity needed if we want to rule out the disorder

---

[68] Note that the qualification "for its own use" refers to the quality Kant calls the principle's "heautonomy" and not to the content of the assumption the principle demands; the assumption is that there is cognizable order *in nature*, not that nature is suitable *for us* (see Section 1.2.2).

(whether rampant or errant) that threatens the claim to necessity of empirical causal laws. Accordingly, an assumption of conceptual order – combined with the Postulates' continued assurance of the "material necessity in existence" (A 226/B 279) of empirical laws of nature – is to provide the transcendental-philosophical warrant for the understanding's business of making possible coherent experience of ourselves and our world.

Kant, to be sure, has not forgotten the hard-won lesson from the Appendix to the Dialectic and insists that the assumption of nature's "thinkable" (CJ, 5:184.01) systematic unity must not be an assumption of *objective* unity:

> This transcendental concept of a purposiveness of nature is neither a concept of nature nor a concept of freedom, since it attributes nothing at all to the object (i.e., nature) but rather only represents the unique way in which we must proceed in reflection on the objects of nature with the aim of a thoroughly interconnected experience, consequently it is a subjective principle (maxim) of the power of judgment. (CJ, 5:184.10–16)

But even allowing that Kant's argument for the transcendental necessity of a principle of nature's systematic unity has evolved (a) from an effort to establish an objective (determining) principle to an effort to establish a subjective (regulative) principle and (b) from an effort to solve a somewhat engineered problem of critical epistemology (the problem of the status of more than merely pragmatically binding heuristic maxims) to an effort to solve a genuine problem of critical epistemology (the problem of the status of the claim to necessity of empirical causal laws) – Kant's argument, as presented, still fails.

The reason is simple. When Kant notes that "as far as one can judge *a priori*" (CJ, 5:183.15–16) the world might be fundamentally chaotic, the standard of judgment he has in mind is the transcendental causal principle. But his point is a perfectly general one. Any a priori principle addressing the systematic unity of nature – whether an objective principle proclaiming nature's de facto unity or a subjective principle demanding, merely, that we approach nature as if systematic unity resided within it – is fully consistent with the possibility that nature is not, after all, systematic. Nature's systematic unity is simply not the sort of thing that can be deduced into existence or whose feared absence can be warded off by a priori guarantees. If nature were fundamentally unsystematic, no transcendental-philosophical assurance to the contrary could alleviate that fact. If, conversely, nature were fundamentally systematic, no transcendental-philosophical assurance that it is indeed so could add to that fact or make nature any more suitable to our cognitive pursuits than, on that hypothesis, it already is. One way or the other, no such assurance can accomplish what it seeks to accomplish and none can, accordingly, be transcendentally necessary.

Epistemology, including critical epistemology, can only be effective at offering solutions to epistemic problems – and a threat of disorder at the objective level is not that. The titular boast of §V of the introduction – that "The Principle of the Formal Purposiveness of Nature is a Transcendental Principle" (CJ, 5:181.13–14) – accordingly, has yet to be redeemed.

Fortunately, there is more to Kant's deduction of a transcendental methodological principle of reflecting judgment than has been apparent so far. Specifically, the noted worry about a world in which there might be "no thoroughgoing interconnection of empirical cognitions into a whole of experience" (CJ, 5:183.30–31) is not simply an expression of the threat of a world supporting conflicting empirical laws of nature. Rather, the threat of non-interconnected cognitions is the first step in Kant's articulation of a distinct epistemic worry about human experience – a worry about a fundamental form of cognitive chaos – that can and must be addressed by a transcendental principle of purposiveness.

## 4 The Transcendental Deduction of the Principle of Nature's Purposiveness

### 4.1 Introduction: Into the Box

The context in which the worry about a fundamental form of cognitive chaos arises is crucial for understanding its character. Despite Kant's seemingly exhaustive discussion of the relation between sensibility and understanding in the *Critique of Pure Reason*, he notes, in the *Critique of the Power of Judgment*, that there is a cognitive task at the intersection of sensible particularity and conceptual universality that is epistemically foundational but that nevertheless cannot be discharged on the model of cognition established in the first *Critique*. As Kant now presents the issue, in negotiating that intersection the understanding is bound to follow a uniform logical direction as it goes *from* the universal *to* the particular in its subsumption of objects under concepts in determining judgments. This leaves the understanding unable to traverse in the opposite direction, going *from* the particular *to* the universal. Kant considers this ascent to the universal a form of "reflection" (CJ, 5:180.14) and he calls judgments engaged in it "reflecting judgments" (CJ, 5:191.21). Since the logical direction of reflecting judgments is the inverse of the understanding's native determining orientation in cognition, Kant assigns reflecting judgments to a new cognitive power with a native direction of its own – the "reflecting power of judgment" (CJ, 5:180.05).

Kant justifies the need for a separate cognitive capacity with the idea that ascending from the particular to the universal is neither incidental to nor optional for human cognition. Instead, it saves our form of cognition from a debilitating kind of chaos that, Kant now holds, a critical epistemology based solely on the principles of determining judgment articulated in the *Critique of Pure Reason* must incur. Despite its late arrival on the critical scene, the reflecting power of judgment accordingly assumes its rightful place, alongside reason and the understanding, in the firmament of the upper cognitive faculties.

Kant's latest considerations about the nature of judgment and Kant's earlier considerations about nature's systematicity converge, moreover, because the principle that is to govern this reflecting power of judgment – and whose role in averting cognitive chaos is at the heart of the ultimately successful version of its transcendental deduction – is a principle of nature's purposiveness.

## 4.2 A Problem of Chaos

### 4.2.1 Empirical Chaos

Kant's first articulation of a threat of chaos among our cognitions comes in the form of the noted worry that, on the counterfactually presumed absence of the principle of nature's purposiveness, "no thoroughgoing interconnection of empirical cognitions into a whole of experience would take place" (CJ, 5:183.30–31). This threat has been fittingly described as a "specter ... of 'empirical chaos'" (Allison, 2001, 38) because it conjures a world of spatiotemporally and at least partially conceptually determined empirical objects that stand in causal commerce with one another but whose interactions are so unsystematic as to afford cognitive agents a, at best, highly disjointed and disorienting form of self-conscious experience. Note, however, that, as a specter of specifically *empirical* chaos, the threat must be rooted in nature and not in the absence of a reflecting orientation in thinking. After all, our powers of synthesization here work just as they should or else they would not yield empirical cognitions at all. This leaves no transcendental-logical reason why those powers' cognitive fruits should resist reliable integration into a system of genera and species. The world conjured is, in other words, transcendental-philosophically consistent – just not a place we should care to visit – and its distinct drawbacks accordingly prove impervious to transcendental philosophical remediation.

In general, cognitive chaos that presupposes a ground-level of successful empirical object-cognition ("empirical chaos") is not a consequence of an epistemic shortfall nor, more specifically, rooted in the absence of a proper cognitive ascent from the particular to the universal. Accordingly, a threat of this type cannot be the premise on which a transcendental deduction that seeks to establish the necessity of such an ascent turns.[69] Either Kant has a different

---

[69] See Teufel (2012, 311–317).

type of cognitive chaos in mind or the deduction, which could not be made to work on the assumption that the threat at issue is the nonnecessity of empirical laws, cannot be made to work on the assumption that the threat at issue is a form of cognitive chaos either.

### 4.2.2 A Problem of Fit

In an indication that Kant's original presentation of the transcendental deduction of the principle of nature's purposiveness leaves something to be desired, Kant starts to revisit it the moment he completes it.[70] And, in revisiting the claims of the deduction, Kant begins to change them in just the ways that make a successful argument possible. Kant not only continues to shift the weight of the deduction from an argument that addresses a threat of the nonnecessity of empirical causal laws to an argument that addresses a threat of the non-interconnectedness of cognitions but, in doing so, begins to shift the identity of the deduction from an argument that addresses a threat rooted in the world to an argument that addresses a threat rooted in critical epistemology itself.

The clearest manifestation of these shifts is that Kant's reformulation of the deduction now puts pressure on the idea that the cognitive chaos at issue already presupposes a ground level of successful empirical object-cognition. Near the end of §V of the Introduction, Kant presents the cognitive threat in question in this way. On the counterfactually presumed absence of the principle of nature's purposiveness:

> The specific diversity of the empirical laws of nature together with their effects could nevertheless be so great that it would be impossible for our understanding to discover in them an order that we can grasp . . . and to make an interconnected experience out of material that is for us so confused (strictly speaking only infinitely manifold and not fitted for our power of comprehension). (CJ, 5:185.26–34)

In this version of the threat, Kant still refers to the "specific diversity" of empirical causal laws as situated at the root of our threatened inability to forge coherent cognition out of the material nature provides. But note, first, that the threat has evolved from one of *not fully* interconnected experience to one of *fully non*-interconnected experience – one on which it would be "impossible" (CJ, 5:185.28) to make interconnected experience. Note, further, that a manifold that is truly "not fitted for our power of comprehension" (CJ, 5:185.32–33), as Kant's parenthetical precisification of the threat now renders it, cannot be a manifold of already epistemically available empirical laws, or

---

[70] See CJ, 5:184.22–24, 185.23.

empirical objects, or even empirical intuitions. After all, any of those *would* be fitted for our power of comprehension, if for no other reason than that all of them would be products of the understanding's syntheses to begin with. A manifold truly not fitted for our power of comprehension – one that fails to provide "an order that we can grasp" (CJ, 5:185.28) – must be a creature of a different sort.

The true nature of the cognitive threat at issue comes into better focus when we realize that – expressed as a problem of fit – it is no longer obvious that the blame for our looming failure "to make an interconnected experience" (CJ, 5:185.33–34) should lie with nature (for serving up material without order); the blame for our looming failure to make an interconnected experience could lie with us (for being unable to find the order in the material nature serves up). And that is, of course, what Kant now says. The scale ("so great") of the "specific diversity of the empirical laws of nature" (CJ, 5:185.26) that Kant invokes to characterize the threat at issue no longer conjures the de facto absence of natural order, as the earlier worry that objects may "still *be* causes in an infinite variety of ways" had (CJ, 5:183.18; my emphasis). On the present scenario, there may very well be such order. The problem is that, in the absence of a transcendental principle of nature's purposiveness, that order would not be "an order that *we* can grasp" (CJ, 5:185.28; my emphasis) because the material that presents it would be "*for us* so confused" (CJ, 5:185.31; my emphasis).

With the onus thus apparently on us, how, exactly, could we go wrong? How can material that, for all we know, contains lawful order nevertheless, "for us," be confused? Even assuming that whatever natural order may be contained in this material were overwhelmingly complex in its "specific diversity," why should it be "impossible" for our understanding to hit upon and to begin to decipher that order, eventually arriving at an evolving scientific picture of the world in question (whatever its limitations) – and, in the process, validating the critical epistemology of the first *Critique* on which that picture is predicated? What could possibly be amiss?

Kant addresses these questions – providing a clearly defined problem in need of a transcendental-philosophical solution – in §§76–77 of the Dialectic of the Teleological Power of Judgment. For now, note that if the material Kant characterizes as infinitely manifold were truly not fitted for our power of comprehension, then it would at a minimum – and ex hypothesi – be material on which our power of comprehension has not (or not yet) been exercised. To consider this infinitely manifold material in that transcendental-logical position is, accordingly, to consider it (as yet) aside from and, hence, unmediated by that cognitive power. But our "power of comprehension" (CJ, 5:185.32) is our power of synthesis. The suggestion in Kant's recapitulation of the rationale for the deduction is, accordingly, that to consider *this* material in *that* position is to consider it aside from and, hence, unmediated by cognitive syntheses. And if that is correct, then the material that Kant characterizes as "strictly speaking only infinitely manifold" (CJ, 5:185.32) must be as yet unsynthesized sensory material.

That critical epistemology should countenance unsynthesized sensory material as logically independent of the processes of synthesization into which it enters is perhaps not surprising. What is surprising – and the philosophical point of Kant's thought-experiment of a counterfactually presumed absence of the principle of nature's purposiveness – is the idea of a fundamental lack of fit between such material and the power of comprehension we bring to it. Taking Kant at his word, then, the sensations he has in mind when he characterizes the material that nature provides for our comprehension as "infinitely manifold" would not only have to be deemed as-yet unsynthesiz*ed*. In the counterfactually presumed absence of a principle of nature's purposiveness that alone is supposed to help us get around that lack of fit, those sensations would – "strictly speaking [*eigentlich*]" (CJ, 5:185.32) – have to be deemed as-yet unsynthesiz*able*.

### 4.2.3 Transcendental Chaos

That we are dealing with a problem at this level of epistemic fundamentality is confirmed when Kant revisits the transcendental deduction of the principle of nature's purposiveness in §76–77 of the teleological Dialectic. Kant revisits the deduction because he still needs to show that the logically singular reflecting judgments that supposedly derive from the transcendental principle of nature's purposiveness are a priori and necessary judgments (lest his aesthetics and tele-ology fail to be duly critical) and so that the conflict between the powers of reflection and determination in our judging of organized beings in nature is a "natural and unavoidable" (CJ, 5:340.27–28) antinomial conflict. A precondition for these things is to return to the unfinished business of the transcendental deduction of the principle of purposiveness and establish that the principle of the reflecting power of judgment is indeed a transcendental principle.

Kant consequently picks up the thread of the problem of fit, left unresolved in §V of the Introduction, in the context of the need to account for the necessity of judging biological organisms teleologically ("the case before us"; CJ, 5:404.17). He begins his renewed discussion of the problem of fit by noting that such judging would not be possible – and so could not be necessary – for our understanding. This is because of a "special character" (CJ, 5:405.02) or "peculiarity" (CJ, 5:406.34) exhibited by our understanding. The peculiarity in question is what we might call our understanding's mero-mechanistic character. It requires us to judge mereological wholes as mechanistic effects of their parts. In §77, Kant explains that this inherent structural constraint on our understanding is the manifestation of the understanding's native determining orientation in thinking. According to that orientation, our thinking is ineluctably directed toward sensible intuition. This direction entails an asymmetry. In its cognition of objects, our thinking must proceed *from* conceptual universals *to* sensible particulars. That, in turn, entails our cognition's mero-mechanism, because sensible intuition "merely give[s] us something without thereby allowing us to cognize it as an object" (CJ, 5:402.04–05). Intuition's nonobjective, sensible "somethings" are instead first cognized *as objects* when we subsume them under concepts of parts that (a) *compose* them (hence, when we judge them *as wholes*) and (b) *cause* them (hence, when we judge those wholes *as effects*).[71]

To say that this is an inherent structural constraint is to say that we cannot turn the process around and start with intuition's nonobjective, sensible somethings in hope of either intuiting sensibly or deriving logically the parts that cause and compose them. We cannot intuit those parts and causes sensibly because cognition of parts and causes is conceptual – and sensible intuiting is not. We cannot derive them logically because conceptually undetermined sensible material does not afford the logical articulation from which such derivation can alone proceed.

Cognition of sensibly given somethings as objects accordingly appears to have to start from a position of *antecedent* conceptualization. Now, if a whole is always antecedently explained – qua whole – as caused and composed by its parts, then the teleological demand for the parts' inverse causal dependence on that whole must (on pain of circularity) become impossible for our understanding to satisfy.[72] But if that is so, then the vexing demands of teleology now appear to be the least of our problems. The idea that determining cognition must always start in medias res – from a position of antecedent conceptualization – because we cannot extract empirical concepts either intuitively or logically from sensation, raises the question how we can possibly come into possession of those concepts in the first place. Perhaps even more troubling, it raises the question how any concepts we may already be in possession of could possibly have cognitive purchase on sensation at all. After all, logically unarticulated sensible material would be fully nonisomorphic to our concepts. As Kant puts this problem of fit at the start of §76, sensible intuition and the understanding's concepts are "two entirely heterogeneous elements" (CJ, 5:401.34) for our cognition.

Kant calls sensible material considered as yet utterly untouched by our synthesizing capacities "the particular, *as such*" (CJ, 5:404.24; my emphasis). This is an assertively *transcendental-logical* notion of particularity, meant to distinguish it from the pedestrian *logical* notion, which refers to already

---

[71] See CJ, 5:407.28–30.    [72] See CJ, 5:407.34–37.

spatiotemporally and conceptually determined empirical objects. Kant's surprising answer to the question about concept formation and concept application, which the mero-mechanistic peculiarity of our understanding raises, is that – in the counterfactually presumed absence of the principle of the reflecting power of judgment – sensible material must remain fully beyond the reach of our conceptual capacities. Kant declares that, with respect to "the particular as such," our understanding alone "determines nothing" (CJ, 5:407.17).

This is an astonishing pronouncement from the author of the *Critique of Pure Reason* this late in the development of critical philosophy: Kant in effect proclaims chaos at the transcendental level. Keenly aware of the high drama, and evidently intent on driving the point home, Kant repeats it three times (see CJ, 5:406.14, 5:406.35, 5:407.17). Whether inspired or misguided, the third *Critique*'s discordant corollary to the first *Critique*'s famous principle that "intuitions without concepts are blind" (A 51/B 75) is that, in the absence of a principle of reflection, intuitions must stay that way.

## 4.3 Intuitive Manifolds

### 4.3.1 Representing Intuitive Manifolds

At this point, the student of the *Critique of Pure Reason* will rightly demand why our synthesizing capacities should be unable to wrest empirical cognition from sensible material. Kant, after all, tells a well-known, comprehensive, and compelling story about just that foundational moment in our cognitive endeavors in the first *Critique*'s Analytic of Concepts under the heading of "On the Synthesis of Apprehension in the Intuition" (A 98), the first and most basic of the three interrelated syntheses he discusses there. To say, as Kant now does, that "the understanding determines nothing with regard to the manifoldness [of the particular of the given empirical intuition]" (CJ, 5:407.15–17) seems directly to contradict his account there.

Fortunately, Kant's analysis in the third *Critique* does not contradict his earlier exploration of the matter. Instead, Kant's analysis turns the critical headlights on the – it turns out – insufficiently probed first premise of that exploration. That crucial first premise states that "Every intuition contains a manifold in itself" (A 99). In the *Critique of Pure Reason*, Kant distinguishes between what we might call a *material* and a *formal* interpretation of this first premise. The *Critique of the Power of Judgment* makes its late contribution to Kant's critical epistemology because the first *Critique* leaves the latter, formal interpretation underdeveloped. Specifically, Kant fails to distinguish, further, between a *preconditional* and a *consequential* dimension of that formal interpretation. The contribution of the third *Critique* can be summed up by saying that Kant's account of the transcendental principle of nature's purposiveness provides the critical-philosophical analysis of the (a) transcendental justification (see Section 4.4.1), (b) claim (see Section 4.4.2), (c) cognitive role (see Sections 4.4.3–4), (d) structure (see Sections 4.4.5–6), and (e) normative status (see Section 4.4.7) of that preconditional dimension of the formal interpretation of "every intuition contains a manifold in itself."

As first proposed at A 99, "every intuition contains a manifold in itself" is a descriptive premise about the sensible material entering into our cognitive syntheses. It announces, as a transcendental but material condition of the possibility of self-conscious human experience, that, unless sensible intuition contained a manifold of re-identifiable features, no cognitive syntheses of such material would be possible.[73] Yet Kant notes that this material condition is insufficient for the possibility of cognition. It must be supplemented by a formal counterpart. He explains that the manifold contained in every intuition "however would not be *represented as such* if the mind did not distinguish the time in the succession of impressions on one another" (A 99; my emphasis). To wit: a manifold of intuition does not an intuition of a manifold make. And not representing a manifold as what it is – a manifold – would mean not cognizing it at all.

The reason why manifolds of intuition do not simply disclose themselves but must first be represented as manifolds is that, "as modifications of the mind" (A 99), manifolds of intuition "belong to inner sense" (A 99) and so are "subjected to the formal condition of inner sense, namely time" (A 99). The elements of such manifolds, accordingly, must be situated in time as well. And unless those elements are "ordered, connected, and brought into relations" (A 99), that is to say, unless we "run through and then … take together this manifoldness" (A 99), a manifold of intuition in time cannot present us with even so much as a disarray of elements – for even that would require that we at least survey (run through) those elements. Rather, an un-run-through manifold of intuition presents us with no elements – hence, with no manifold – at all. An un-run-through intuitive manifold, to us, cannot be an undifferentiated many, it must be a hermetic, unbounded one: an "absolute unity" (A 99).

Now, fortunately, "running through" and "taking together" the elements of an intuitive manifold are spontaneous synthetic activities of the transcendental imagination. Given this cognitive automatism, Kant, in the *Critique of Pure Reason*, sees no further philosophical difficulty with the way in which we avail ourselves of the perspective on manifolds of intuition that our cognitive syntheses of those manifolds require – we run through, take together, and, so, do represent them as manifolds. Through the spontaneity of our syntheses

---

[73] See Westphal (2004, 118–122).

(combined with the material condition mentioned), the threat of confronting sensible material that, for us, would remain hermetically sealed is accordingly warded off, the basic isomorphism of intuitions and concepts (i.e., intuition's provision of re-identifiable elements ready for cognitive uptake) is ascertained, and the road cleared for our synthetic labors to bear their cognitive fruits.

### 4.3.2 Representing Intuitive Manifolds as Manifolds

Kant's aim in the *Critique of the Power of Judgment* is not to change this basic account of the synthesis of apprehension but to make its internal logic and transcendental justification more fully transparent. Specifically, Kant seeks to unravel the sheer duplicative oddity of the demand to represent a kind of representation (an intuitive manifold) *as* that kind of representation (an intuitive manifold). The central takeaway from this renewed focus on the foundations of our cognitive syntheses is that the cognitively indispensable representation of an intuitive manifold as manifold, however inseparably connected it may be to the understanding's syntheses, is not itself a synthesis of the understanding but a different kind of representing assigned to a cognitive power of its own.

For there is a curious circularity at the heart of Kant's account of the synthesis of apprehension in the Analytic of Concepts. What first avails us of the vantage point from which intuitive manifolds can be represented as manifolds – hence, as synthesizable – is the *synthetic* act of "running through and taking together" their elements. We must synthesize before we can ascertain synthesizability. There would be nothing so very wrong with such a spontaneous leap into the unknown if it were not for the fact that the leap itself presupposes just what it is supposed to allow us to claim. The structure of determining syntheses enshrines an assumption, not warranted by the transcendental-logical position in which we encounter un-run-through intuitive manifolds – as absolute unities – namely that they are *not* absolute unities. Specifically, the multi-place relational structure of determining syntheses as a *running from_through_to_* and as a *taking_together with_as_* presupposes runable-through and takeable-together – hence, *synthesizable* – material available to enter into that structure. The Analytic of Concepts, in short, wants to have it both ways. We must first run through and take together intuitive manifolds in order to be able to represent them as manifolds *and* we must first represent intuitive manifolds as manifolds in order to be able to run through and take them together.

Fortunately, this circularity is not vicious, because the de facto synthesizability of the sensible material we ascertain in and through successful synthetic activity is not the same as the merely *presupposed* synthesizability that is required in order to engage in that activity in the first place. Kant's account in the Analytic of Concepts is logically sound – and escapes transcendental chaos – so long as we distinguish two ways of representing intuitive manifolds as manifolds: (a) as a *precondition for* our cognitive syntheses, (b) as a *consequence of* our cognitive syntheses. In the *Critique of Pure Reason*, Kant is principally concerned with the latter, less problematic representation. The transcendental-logical thrust of the third *Critique* is the identification, analysis, and justification of the former, more problematic one.

What kind of representation, then, is this preconditional representation of intuitive manifolds as manifolds? Minimally, it is an assumption that re-identifiable *relata* are available to enter into the multi-place relational structure of our cognitive syntheses. But this cannot be a descriptive assumption that construes those *relata* as objects. After all, *that* would be a form of determination, and all determination instead presupposes the assumption. If the preconditional representation of intuitive manifolds as manifolds is a determination at all, it can then only be a structural determination of the *form* of synthesis in and through which those manifolds first disclose themselves as manifolds to us.

This determination of the structure of determination is ex hypothesi neither a sensible intuition nor a determining synthesis. By the antipodal lights of the *Critique of Pure Reason*, the preconditional representation of intuitive manifolds as manifolds must then be a cognitive orphan in search of both a home and transcendental warrant. In the *Critique of the Power of Judgment* Kant stands poised to offer both.

## 4.4 The Transcendental Principle of Nature's Purposiveness

The transcendental-philosophical warrant for the assumption – inscribed into the multi-place relational structure of our cognitive syntheses – that re-identifiable sensible *relata* are available to enter into that structure is straightforward. To cognize in terms of multi-place relational structures and to assume that re-identifiable elements are available to enter into those structures are two sides of the same coin. The assumption is not merely expressive but constitutive of the cognitive structure in which token syntheses are attained. Were cognitive syntheses not so characterized – were an assumption of the availability of re-identifiable elements not reflected in their structure – then they would not *be* cognitive syntheses; there would then be no combinatorial acts of cognition at all.

### 4.4.1 The Deduction

In his tightly woven restatement of the transcendental deduction of the principle of nature's purposiveness in §77, Kant exploits the effective identity between that principle and reflecting a priori judgments of purposiveness (see Section 5.4.4) by addressing both (a) the foundational epistemic case and (b) the biological "case before us" (CJ, 5:404.17) – at the same time. We will need to keep the identity in mind but the strands apart. Kant's argument begins by noting the deep cognitive need for our synthesizing mind to contravene its mero-mechanistic constraint so as "to represent the possibility of the parts as depending on the whole" (CJ, 5:407.32–34). For the foundational epistemic case [(a)], this is the need to go *from* the intuitive manifoldness of a sensible "something" *to* concepts of its parts and causes. This "ascent" is at the root of our cognition of *intuitive* wholes as *compositional, etiological* wholes – of sensible "somethings" as objects. Yet, remarks Kant, while such an ascent may be possible for an understanding that can proceed from "the intuition of a whole as such" (CJ, 5:407.21–22), this cannot be how our own understanding proceeds. After all, in the absence of a preconditional representation of intuitive manifolds as manifolds, our understanding "determines nothing" in the "particular as such," whence an un-run-through "intuition of a whole as such" must, for us, remain "absolute unity" (A 99). How, then, *do* we get around our mero-mechanistic limitation?

In the major premise of the revised transcendental deduction of the principle of nature's purposiveness, Kant explains that we can do this "only [in such a way] that the *representation* of a whole contains the ground of the possibility of its form and of the connection of parts that belongs to that" (CJ, 5:407.37–408.02, my emphasis). For the foundational epistemic case, this means that if we did not approach an un-run-through "intuition of a whole as such" with the assumption that it is grounded in its representation – hence, with the assumption that it exhibits representational articulation – then we could not represent its "form" as manifoldness at all (since that representation of its form is neither an intuition nor a conceptual determination). And if we did not represent its form as manifoldness – in an assumption that accordingly proves to be constitutive of the nature of synthetic labor itself – then we could not put our mero-mechanistic understanding on the path toward representing that intuitive whole as a compositional, etiological whole either. But we *do* represent intuitive wholes as compositional, etiological wholes; our understanding, happily, does *not* "determine ... nothing" (CJ, 5:407.17) in "the particular as such." Accordingly, we must so represent their form as well.[74]

### 4.4.2 Purposiveness

The preconditional representation of intuitive manifolds as exhibiting representational articulation is the assumption of a fundamental isomorphism between

---

[74] For the biological "case before us," this means that we must presuppose "the idea of a whole on which even the constitution and mode of action of the parts depends, which is just how we must represent an organized body" (CJ, 5:408.29–31; see Section 5.4.4).

concepts and intuitions. It is the assumption of the presence, in the sensible material, of re-identifiable features available for synthetic uptake. The moment of re-identifiability is central to Kant's point. The assumption construes the sensible material as containing features that – in light of perduring and shared characteristics – can be "taken together *as*" something or other. It is thus an assumption that at least a modicum of extramental order resides in the sensible material itself. This assumption remains duly nondogmatic since it is a determination of the structure of determining synthesis itself rather than a determining assumption about (or a speculative determination of) supersensible reality.[75] The assumption nevertheless does have objective import, if at a remove; and that import is thinkable for our intellects (and, so, expressible for transcendental philosophy) only through the idea that the order so presumed has causal antecedents in structuring concepts. It is, in short, thinkable and expressible only as the idea of nature's purposiveness.

For our synthesizing minds, then, conceptual structure is always presupposed. This is not the same as to say that our cognitive efforts start in medias res, among preexistent conceptualizations. It is, rather, to say that a foundational reflecting assumption of inexistent conceptual order in the sensible material vaults us into the only position from which downstream conceptualizations of that material become possible for us. The presupposition of conceptual structure accordingly allows us to ascend from "the particular as such" (i.e., from unsynthesized sensible material considered *un*synthesizable) to the universal *as such* (i.e., to a realm of conceptualization in which even as-yet-unsynthesized sensible material is nevertheless already deemed synthesizable; or, in Kant's useful phrase, to a realm of "cognition overall"; CJ, 5:217.20).

### 4.4.3 Reflecting

Kant considers this a priori ascent from the particular (as such) to the universal (as such) a form of reflection – and the power of judgment that performs that ascent the reflecting power of judgment – because it shares an important dimension with ordinary a posteriori forms of reflection. Specifically, both a priori and a posteriori forms of reflection involve adopting a cognitive posture toward their object as a condition of its conceptual determination. The difference is that, in the case of a posteriori reflection, the candidate for determination is an already spatiotemporally and conceptually determined object. The reflection at issue is accordingly a form of ex post facto deliberation or self-conscious "thinking about" that object. In the case of the reflecting power of judgment's a priori reflection, by contrast, the candidate for determination is sensible

---

[75] It, moreover, continues to be complemented by its "material" counterpart (see Section 4.3.1).

particularity itself – and the reflection at issue names a transcendentally necessary, subpersonal cognitive orientation toward it.

A posteriori forms of reflection (including empirical, concept-forming syntheses) are consequently *not* exercises of the new reflecting power of judgment – even as they presuppose it – but continue to be what Kant had considered them all along: token acts of the understanding.[76] Conversely, the reflecting power of judgment's a priori reflection is consequently *not* a form of ex post facto deliberation. It is nevertheless important to stress that, since it is coeval with the spontaneity of our cognitive synthesizing, a priori reflection characterizes an ongoing, foundational orientation toward the world. While that orientation's assumption of nature's purposiveness typically does not itself register in phenomenal consciousness, it remains the key that opens access to a world of conceptually determinable objects for us. Or, as Kant puts it in a passage quoted before: "this transcendental concept of a purposiveness of nature is neither a concept of nature nor a concept of freedom, since it attributes nothing at all to the object (nature) but rather only represents the unique way in which we must proceed in reflection on the objects of nature" (CJ, 5:184.10–15).

### 4.4.4 Regulating

Kant's reference to the principle of nature's purposiveness as representing a "way in which we must proceed" (CJ, 5:184.13–14) highlights the principle's methodological character, central not only to its foundational epistemic role but – crucially – to its additional resonance in aesthetic and biological contexts. According to this methodological character, a priori reflection on nature is a form of cognitive conduct, a rational activity our synthesizing minds must be engaged in. This complicates Kant's doctrine of the spontaneity of our syntheses because this activity is not something we simply happen to engage in. Proceeding in a way in which we must proceed is autonomous, hence, rule-governed or principled action. The principle that "represents the unique way in which we must proceed in reflection on the objects of nature" (CJ, 5:184.13–14) – and that we must *adopt* to so proceed – is accordingly fundamentally practical: it is "a subjective principle (maxim)" (CJ, 5:184.15–16).

The unusual feature of the conduct in question is that the end pursued (namely to attain a cognitive position from which it becomes possible to synthesize sensible material) is a structural end we pursue by dint of being cognitive agents in the first place; it is a necessary end of cognition (arguably, *the* necessary end of cognition). Acting in accordance with the principle that represents the sole and apposite means

---

[76] JL, 9:94.20.

to that necessary end (namely assuming that sensible *relata* are available to enter into our syntheses) is then something that we – of transcendental necessity – must do.

One might think that, for want of volitional contingency in its adoption, this subpersonal cognitive orientation toward the sensible material is no methodological "stance" at all. Kant disagrees. One of the central lessons of the third *Critique* is that a principle can have a subjective domain (that is to say, it can be a regulative or judgment-determining – as opposed to object-determining – principle) without being subjective in its bindingness (that is to say, it can be a technically-practically or even transcendentally necessary principle, rather than a merely heuristic one). All heuristic principles are regulative. Not all regulative principles are heuristic.

### 4.4.5 An Assumption *That Determines Determining Judgment*

The assumption that re-identifiable sensible *relata* are available to enter into our cognitive syntheses is inscribed into the multi-place relational structure of those syntheses and so is constitutive of that structure. The combinatorial structure so determined, which allows us to *take_together with_as_*, is characteristic of predicative cognitive judgments. Consequently, the assumption in question is a regulative or judgment-determining assumption, in contrast to an object-determining assumption. The assumption in question, more specifically, determines *determining* judgment.

As a condition of the possibility of determining syntheses, this assumption cannot itself be a determining synthesis. It is, however, not therefore noncognitive. Kant accordingly assigns the capacity to be so oriented toward the sensible material – and, in consequence, to determine the nature and structure of determining judgment – to the independent, if previously unsung, reflecting power of judgment.

### 4.4.6 A Demand *That Determines Reflecting Judgment*

As presented thus far, the transcendental deduction of the principle of nature's purposiveness establishes two main points. First, in order to be able to synthesize sensible material, we must assume that re-identifiable sensible *relata* are available to enter into those syntheses. Second, this assumption must be made by the reflecting power of judgment. The methodological character of the transcendental principle of nature's purposiveness entails a third point. Qua maxim governing cognitive conduct, the principle of nature's purposiveness *demands* that the reflecting power of judgment make that assumption. To the extent that the reflecting power of judgment abides by that demand (which is to say, wholly, since – of transcendental necessity – it must), the reflecting power of judgment is accordingly governed by it. That reveals a curious structural duality. While the assumption demanded determines the determining power of judgment, the demand to so assume determines the reflecting power of judgment.

### 4.4.7 Heautonomy

This brings us to the final and arguably most important feature of the transcendental principle of nature's purposiveness: its "heautonomy" (CJ, 5:185.37) or *self*-governance.[77] At this point, we understand the governance of the transcendental principle of nature's purposiveness reasonably well. The transcendental deduction of that principle tells us that our synthesizing minds must abide by a demand (that determines the reflecting power of judgment) to make an assumption (that determines the determining power of judgment). We also know that the source of this "demand for an assumption" can neither be the understanding (because the understanding's syntheses presuppose it) nor reason (because there is no basis in reason for a principle of this kind).

Neither a principle of reason nor a principle of the understanding, what kind of principle is it? Qua principle that governs the power of judgment, it is a regulative principle and so falls broadly in the domain of the judgment-governing reflecting power of judgment. But the power of judgment it governs is, here, the reflecting power of judgment *itself*. It is, in other words, a principle both *of* and *for* the reflecting power of judgment. Kant says, "The power of judgment thus also has in itself an *a priori* principle for the possibility of nature, though only in a subjective respect, by means of which it prescribes a law, not to nature (as autonomy) but to itself (as heautonomy) for reflection on nature" (CJ, 5:185.35–186.01).

The concept of heautonomy captures a scenario on which, in Schiller's gloss, a rule "is at once given and obeyed by the thing" (Schiller 2003, 167). Contrary to appearances, this form of self-determination does not entail a fatal form of circularity. To see why, consider that any exercise of the reflecting power of judgment must be governed by some subjective (i.e., regulative or judgment-determining) principle or other. Typically, those are maxims by means of which the reflecting power of judgment governs – and so determines – the determining power of judgment. Central examples of this form of governance are the (more than merely pragmatic) methodological principles of natural science – such as "*natura non facit saltus*"[78] – by means of which the reflecting power of judgment instructs the determining power of judgment how to proceed in

---

[77] "Heautonomy" is a Kantian neologism, a portmanteau of the Greek reflexive pronoun *heautou* (*of him-*, *her-*, *itself*) and *nomos* (*law*).

[78] This, of course, *remains* a heuristic desideratum of reason, despite Kant's inability to prove nature's maximal continuity (see Section 3.2.1).

scientific inquiry. Additional examples are regulative maxims that have an even stronger (more than merely heuristic) form of bindingness, such as the maxim of mechanistic judging at the heart of the teleological antinomy (whose sufficiency for judging causal origins in nature is there in dispute, even as its technical-practical necessity for so judging is not). Crucially, in all of these cases, the reflecting power of judgment adopts the law by means of which it governs determining judgments of nature autonomously or unconstrained by psychological automatisms or other extraneous limitations.

The same holds true for the adoption of the principle of nature's purposiveness. The case of that principle is different because of (a) its peculiar form of bindingness (it is transcendentally necessary), (b) the form of judging so bound (it determines reflecting judgment). Regarding this second difference, we must then distinguish between the exercise of the reflecting power of judgment involved in *adopting* the law (Schiller's "giving") and the exercise of the reflecting power of judgment involved in *abiding by* the law so adopted (Schiller's "obeying"). The latter, specific, transcendentally necessary exercise (namely assuming the availability of re-identifiable *relata* in the sensible material) is separate from the former, generic one (namely adopting a law). The specific law adopted does not govern the faculty's generic ability to adopt laws – including this one – even as the tasks of giving and obeying it are thus discharged by the same faculty. Accordingly, the foundational autonomy of the adoption of that law is not subverted by the law's transcendental necessity. After all, heteronomy is a measure of the source of a principle, not of the strength of its bindingness. And, qua regulative principle, the principle of nature's purposiveness is very much a principle *of* (if also *for*) the reflecting power of judgment. Heautonomy, or the *self-giving* of a *self-governing* law, is accordingly not only not a self-contradictory exercise of our power of judgment but a bona fide form of autonomy.

It is also cognitive and normative bedrock. The heautonomy of the transcendental principle of nature's purposiveness captures a foundational cognitive stance our power of judgment – of transcendental necessity – must take toward the sensible material. Because this posture is struck in and coeval with our spontaneous synthesizing, our power of judgment is primordially and ongoingly oriented toward the world in this way: continuously demanding of itself to assume the world's inexistent conceptual order and hence its purposiveness. The ingenious and gently subversive idea behind Kant's discussion of aesthetic and teleological phenomena in the body of the *Critique of the Power of Judgment* is that these phenomena strike us when the world *fails* to answer that hopeful call.

# 5 Nature's *Saltūs*

## 5.1 Introduction: Inside the Box

The transcendental deduction of the principle of nature's purposiveness presents the principal exegetical hurdle to understanding Kant's critical teleological philosophy in the *Critique of the Power of Judgment*. But while unearthing Kant's argument requires a certain degree of forensic élan, Kant does say a fair bit about the matter, leaving plenty of clues over the course of the book to sustain our interpretative efforts and to allow us to attribute a coherent story to him. The textual pickings are less rich when we turn to the exegetical difficulty that plays runner-up: how the transcendental principle so deduced might relate to the two kinds of judgment it supposedly governs – reflecting aesthetic judgments and reflecting teleological judgments. Kant says next to nothing about the nature of the connection between the supreme principle of the reflecting power of judgment and the reflecting judgments that belong to that power. This is why, on that score, I have referred to Kant's third *Critique* as a black box.

Yet the structure of Kant's critical teleology not only commits him to the notion that there must be such a connection, Kant moreover seems to think he has established it. Specifically, Kant believes that the apriority and necessity of the principle of nature's purposiveness explains the apriority and necessity of reflecting aesthetic and reflecting teleological judgments. Consider the aesthetic case. In the lead-up to the deduction of judgments of taste in the Analytic of the Aesthetic Power of Judgment, Kant, as we saw, stresses the apriority of first-order reflecting aesthetic judgments. This creates a problem for transcendental philosophy. My judgment that something is beautiful cannot be the same sort of a priori judgment as my judgment that something is a causally interacting substance in space and time. The latter is true of all objects of possible experience; the former, thankfully, is not. Neither an a priori and universal determining judgment nor an a posteriori and singular determining judgment (merely backed by a priori principles) – but, instead, an a priori and singular reflecting judgment – what kind of judgment is it? That is the question the transcendental principle of the reflecting power of judgment now comes on the scene to resolve. Kant says: "This problem thus concerns the a priori principles of the pure power of judgment *in* aesthetic judgments" (CJ, 5:288.22–23; my emphasis);[79] and he says much the same thing concerning the apriority of teleological judgments in the Analytic of the Teleological Power of Judgment.[80] Kant's point is this: In the context of the third *Critique*, the apriority and necessity of a priori reflecting judgments of

---

[79] See Allison (2001, 173).     [80] See CJ, 5:376.17–22.

a "purposiveness without purpose" and of a priori reflecting judgments of a "purposiveness with purpose" somehow *just is* the apriority and necessity of the principle of nature's purposiveness.

But if that is the position, then why such a dearth of explicit doctrine? Why does Kant not reveal the rationale – so different from his account of the a priori dimension of ordinary empirical judgments – by which reflecting aesthetic and reflecting teleological judgments, connected to an a priori principle of nature's purposiveness, can be both epistemically a priori and logically singular at the same time? The cynic (or realist?) will say that Kant does not offer such an account because there is none to offer: the proposed combination of epistemic apriority and logical singularity makes Kant's aspirations for a theory of reflecting judgment of either flavor patently incoherent; we should content ourselves with trying to salvage the wealth of local aesthetic and teleological insights the third *Critique* has to offer and stop chasing pipe dreams of a unified account. On the flip side of this, there is a view Kant may very well have subscribed to himself, roughly, that the connection between the a priori principle of purposiveness and a priori judgments of purposiveness is so obvious that it would be redundant to spell it out.

I suspect the truth lies somewhere in the middle. The combination of epistemic and logical characteristics of a priori reflecting judgments of purposiveness is indeed inconsistent by the standards of the *Critique of Pure Reason*. This makes Kant reluctant to address the matter in broad daylight, so to speak, and leads him to decline wading deeper into the systemic changes to critical doctrine his account of reflecting judgment entails than he is prepared to in a book that seems happy to downplay rather than to advertise its iconoclasms. By the same token, once the transcendental principle at the root of these changes is properly understood, we can see with relative ease how reflecting aesthetic judgments and reflecting teleological judgments with just those characteristics must flow from it.

## 5.2 Rules of Engagement

Kant opens the Critique of the Teleological Power of Judgment with a section "On the Objective Purposiveness of Nature" (CJ, 5:359.02; §61) that precedes both the teleological Analytic and the teleological Dialectic. In it, Kant introduces the central difficulty that will occupy him for the rest of the teleology: the question of the justificatory and objective grounds of teleological judgments of organized beings in nature.

The upshot of Kant's introductory stab at the matter is negative: Kant seeks to define the nature of the problem and to delimit the range of possible solutions; Kant in effect lays down the rules of engagement for the clash between reflection and determination that is to come. Consistent with his subsequent position in the teleological Analytic, Kant does not dispute the legitimacy of our teleological estimation of certain products of nature nor (as the title of the section indicates) the objective import of that estimation. Yet, consistent with both the thesis and the antithesis in the "Antinomy of the Power of Judgment" (CJ, 5:385.04) in the teleological Dialectic – both of which are fully committed to the universal necessity of causal mechanism for explaining origins in nature (including biological origins; leaving only the universal sufficiency of mechanistic judging in dispute) – Kant insists that this objective import cannot have a ground in the sensible nature of things.[81] As Kant puts the point, for the notion "that things of nature serve one another as means to purposes, and that their possibility itself should be adequately intelligible only through this kind of [N.B.: purposive] causality, for that we have no basis at all in the general idea of nature as the sum of the objects of the senses" (CJ, 5:359.14–17). He then divides this "general idea" into its two components, noting that teleological judging has neither an a priori nor an empirical basis.

Concerning an a priori basis, Kant explains that – in the counterfactually presumed absence of an a priori principle of nature's purposiveness – "we have no basis at all for presuming *a priori* that purposes that are not our own, and which also cannot pertain to nature (which we cannot assume as an intelligent being), nevertheless can or should constitute a special kind of causality, or at least an entirely unique lawlikeness thereof" (CJ, 5:359.20–25). Concerning an empirical basis, Kant notes that "even experience cannot prove the reality of this to us unless it has been preceded by some sophistry that has merely projected the concept of the purpose into the nature of things" (CJ, 5:359.25–360.1). This is hardly surprising, given that Kant's position, from the outset, had been that we can have no observational evidence of a purportedly teleological property "since such a property cannot be perceived" (CJ, 5:189.21–22).

The moral of the opening section of Kant's critical philosophy of biology could not be clearer: unless we aim to deceive ourselves, function ascriptions to biological phenomena can have no basis at all in either the a priori conditions of the possibility of experience presented in the *Critique of Pure Reason* or in any actual experience formed in accordance with those conditions. And lest one think that Kant means to relax those conditions themselves (he doesn't), he declares categorically in the teleological Dialectic that "it is absolutely impossible for us to draw from nature itself *any* explanatory grounds for purposive connections" (CJ, 5:410.07–09; my emphasis). A strange position, to be sure, unless you are a fictionalist about

---

[81]  See Teufel (2011b, 202–203).

functions (he is not). It is nevertheless surprising how insistently Kant's interpreters have – in spite of it – sought to draw just such explanatory grounds "from nature itself" and to anchor teleological judgments in some-how nonmechanistic[82] yet nevertheless categorially permissible and experi-entially available[83] forms of causality.

## 5.3 The Analytic: The Predicative Holism of Judgments of Natural Purposes

The Analytic of the Teleological Power of Judgment[84] makes two central contri-butions to Kant's discussion, one positive, the other negative. Positively, the teleological Analytic explains that, when making a reflecting teleological judg-ment of a product of nature, we find ourselves compelled to attribute purposive-ness to "everything that lies in its product" (CJ, 5:377.9–10) and, hence, that "there is no ground for assuming that the form of such a thing is only partially dependent" (CJ, 5:377.13–14) on purposive causality. As a phenomenological consequence of this predicative holism, we judge the parts and properties of the object in question to stand in reciprocal means–end relations with the whole and with each other: "everything in it must be considered as organized, and everything is also, in a certain relation to the thing itself, an organ in turn" (CJ, 5:377.21–23). Kant succinctly encapsulates this biological teleology in the concept of a "natural purpose" (CJ, 5:370.31), a notion that foreshadows the teleological tensions Darwin invites (but, unlike Kant, never fully resolves) only three quarters of a century later in the *Origin of Species*' concept of natural selection.[85]

Negatively, the teleological Analytic functions as a reductio ad absurdum of our intuitive ambition to ground our functional estimation of biological organ-isms in empirical properties – by showing that the reciprocal means–end causality we attribute to organisms in teleological judgments is neither catego-rially permissible nor experientially available nor, therefore, a knowable form of causality at all.

## 5.4 The Dialectic: The Supersensible

### 5.4.1 Supersensible Desperation

Kant's answer to the question of the ground of teleological judgments first takes shape in §66, near the end of the teleological Analytic. Kant there notes that, in the absence of a categorially sanctioned (a priori) or sensibly given (empirical)

---

[82] See McLaughlin (1990, 153; 2003, 214–215), Allison (2003, 221), Ginsborg (2004, 33, 52), Quarfood (2004, 201), Guyer (2005, 354), Zuckert (2007, 101–104), Watkins (2009, 213).

[83] See McLaughlin (1990, 173–174), Ginsborg (2001, 238–239, 243), Zammito (2006, 765).

[84] See CJ, §§62–68.    [85] McLaughlin (2001, 160–161, 190).

ground for our teleological judgments of organized beings, we must instead "relate such an effect [N.B.: such a product of nature] in the whole to a supersensible determining ground" (CJ, 5:377.10–12). Or, as he later puts it "for outer objects as appearances a sufficient ground related to purposes cannot even be found, but this [N.B.: ground], which also lies in nature, must nevertheless be sought only in its supersensible substratum, of which all possible insight is however cut off for us" (CJ, 5:410.03–07).[86]

At first sight, pulling this supersensible rabbit out of the transcendental-philosophical hat seems to be a transparently desperate move on Kant's part, as he is running out of explanatory options near the end of a fast-closing book, the critical wagon careening perilously close to the typesetter's – and the functional fictionalist's – cliff. In fact, more than desperate in a merely hand-waving sort of way, the move seems to court open inconsistency with Kant's official account of the supersensible in the third *Critique*.

### 5.4.2 *Purposiveness, the Supersensible, and the* Provision *of Determinability*

That official account establishes a straightforward relation between the "super-sensible ground" (CJ, 5:413.14–15) of nature and the principle of nature's purposiveness. The notion of "the supersensible," according to Kant, is the principle "on which we must base nature as phenomenon" (CJ, 5:412.35–36). The supersensible is the "substratum" (CJ, 5:410.06) of the phenomenal, sensible world. Kant characterizes this supersensible substratum as "the being in itself of which we know only the appearance" (CJ, 5:422.13–14). Serving as the ground that we must postulate for our sensations, the supersensible thus serves as the ground, also, for any conceptual determinations of those sensations or as the "ground that makes the judging of nature in accordance with empirical laws possible" (CJ, 5:412.14–15).

But, as we saw, the supersensible does not automatically or passively disclose "nature as phenomenon" to us. Instead, Kant's position in the third *Critique* is that the transcendental principle of nature's purposiveness first sets the conditions for the supersensible to play that role. Nowhere does Kant present this

---

[86] This is the antecedent of a conditional claim whose consequent holds that to seek such a ground in nature's supersensible substratum is to locate it in an "original understanding" (CJ, 5:410.11). Note that Kant does not here appeal to an original understanding in order to reframe his own critical "physical teleology" (CJ, 5:442.06) as a "physicotheology" (CJ, 5:442.12). Kant thinks that *that* would be a mistake (see CJ, 5:442.06; see also note 12). Instead, the appeal concludes his discussion in §77, where Kant, among other things, prepares his subsequent regulative "ethicotheology" (CJ, 5:442.12) by offering it as a natural *extension* of his critical teleology: contemplating our own ectypal limitations we are "led to that idea (of an *intellectus archetypus*)" (CJ, 5:408.22–23).

relation between the supersensible ground of nature and the principle of nature's purposiveness more clearly or more authoritatively than in his conclusion concerning the cognitive role of the reflecting power of judgment at the end of the Introduction of the third *Critique*, where he explains the division of labor between the understanding, the power of judgment, and reason. Kant says: "the power of judgment through its *a priori* principle for judging nature in accordance with possible particular laws for it" (CJ, 5:196.15–17) – that is to say, through its heautonomous "demand for an assumption" of nature's inexistent conceptual order – "provides for [nature's] supersensible substratum (in us as well as outside of us) *determinability through the intellectual faculty*" (CJ, 5:196.15–18; Kant's emphasis). More simply: The principle of nature's purposiveness provides (the conditions of) determinability for the supersensible.[87]

Specifically, through its preconditional representation of intuitive manifolds as manifolds, the transcendental principle of nature's purposiveness offers an intellect like our own – whose cognition is based on impressions or images (hence, an "*intellectus ectypus*"; CJ, 5:408.21) – the vantage point from which the material that supersensible nature provides first becomes sensible material. It thus first turns supersensible nature into a ground of determinable impressions, or *ectypoi*, for us. While this does not license determinations of the supersensible ground itself (ex hypothesi, only sensible material can be determined), it does provide determinability for the "appearance" (CJ, 5:422.14) of that ground and so, however indirectly, for "the being" (CJ, 5:422.14) it is the appearance of.

### 5.4.3 Purposiveness, the Supersensible, and the Denial of Determinability

But if that is the official relation the third *Critique* establishes between supersensible reality and the principle of nature's purposiveness, then it appears to have little if anything in common with the relation Kant now proposes to help explain our teleological judgments of biological phenomena. Kant, to be sure, suggests that there is a deep connection. He says that in a priori reflecting attributions of purposiveness to biological phenomena "the cause of the possibility of such a predicate [N.B.: of the concept of a natural purpose]" (CJ, 5:405.10–11) is the same as in the foundational epistemic case. There, the ground of the concept of purposiveness was the transcendental necessity of an assumption of nature's inexistent conceptual order – which, for us, is thinkable only on the model of conceptual causality. And if that is the ground of the concept of purposiveness, also, in our judgments of biological phenomena, then

---

[87] See also CJ, 5:346.17–18.

those judgments must, in their own way, be exercises of the transcendental principle of nature's purposiveness, just as the structure of Kant's account demands. The problem is that, in these exercises, the principle of nature's purposiveness now reveals something entirely different about the supersensible than in the foundational epistemic case.

For in the biological as well as in the aesthetic case, an exercise of the principle of nature's purposiveness does not mark the supersensible as the ground of our *ability* to arrive at determinate cognitions of nature through empirical concepts and laws; to the contrary, an exercise of the principle of nature's purposiveness here marks the supersensible as the ground of our *inability* to arrive at determinate cognitions of nature through empirical concepts and laws. The principle of nature's purposiveness here does not provide determinability for the supersensible by revealing it as the "ground that makes the judging of nature in accordance with empirical laws possible" (CJ, 5:412.14–15); to the contrary, it denies such determinability to the supersensible by revealing it as the ground of judgments that have "no basis at all in the general idea of nature as the sum of the objects of the senses" (CJ, 5:359.14–17). In short, the supersensible, as rendered by an exercise of the principle of nature's purposiveness, is here not the unknowable ground of empirical knowability; to the contrary, it is the unknowable ground of empirical unknowability.[88]

The respective exercises of the principle of nature's purposiveness also appear to have little in common formally, or in the way in which they assume their cognitive roles. Rather than an ongoing subpersonal orientation toward the world (one that provides determinability to the supersensible), an exercise of the principle of purposiveness in the biological and aesthetic cases is a conscious token act (somehow occasioned by a supersensible ground to which such determinability is expressly denied).

Given these discrepancies, Kant's claim that, in the absence of empirical warrant, the "sufficient ground" (CJ, 5:410.04) for our teleological estimation of organic beings "must be sought in [nature's] supersensible substratum" (CJ, 5:410.06) appears to be theoretically adrift; a Hail Mary pass with no discernible – or at least no articulated – relation to the theoretical framework of the book. In the absence of a proper account, the prospect that Kant's aesthetics and philosophy of biology are failed projects in critical philosophy now seems a hair's breadth away from reality.

---

[88] See CJ, 5:346.15–18.

### 5.4.4 Supersensible Solution: Heautonomy and Nature's Saltūs

But just as the situation begins to look dire for Kant's mature teleological philosophy, a solution begins to take shape. It lies in the peculiar way in which, in the biological and in the aesthetic case, the heautonomy of the transcendental principle of nature's purposiveness resonates with the indeterminability of the supersensible.

As we saw, the reflecting power of judgment "provides ... determinability" (CJ, 5:196.15–18) for nature's supersensible substratum through the self-givenness (autonomy) of the a priori self-governance (heautonomy) of the principle of nature's purposiveness. As we also saw, since the self-given self-governance of the principle's demand for an assumption of nature's purposiveness is coeval with the spontaneity of our synthesizing, its provision of (the conditions of) determinability for the supersensible is not only transcendentally necessary but ongoing. It is a primordial orientation toward the world that must obtain regardless of whether the supersensible proves to be responsive to its call.

Now, ex hypothesi, the supersensible is *unresponsive* in the biological and in the aesthetic case: here the principle's demand for an assumption of nature's purposiveness cannot be rewarded by nature's determinability precisely because both cases are marked by the unavailability – in principle – of empirically determinable *ectypoi*. But unrequited love is still love (perhaps its purest form) and the principle's demand for an assumption that ordinarily provides determinability for the supersensible does not cease simply because in this case no determinability is provided.

Stepping back: An aspect of supersensible reality for which no phenomenal appearance is in principle available – despite the ongoing operation of the principle of nature's purposiveness that sets the conditions to make it available – would be an in-principle uncognizable aspect of the world; a *saltus* of just the sort Kant's failed attempt at an objective grounding of *"natura non facit saltus"* sought to rule out. Turning first-*Critique* lemons into third-*Critique* lemonade, Kant now leverages the consequent metaphysical possibility and rational permissibility of nature's leaps for a critical theory of a priori reflecting aesthetic judgments and a priori reflecting teleological judgments – by exploring just what an encounter with such a *saltus* would look like.

Kant's position – as dictated by the structure of his account – is that, in cases where the preconditional representation of intuitive manifolds as manifolds unaccountably fails to provide determinability for the supersensible, we are left with a cognitive void filled only by the reflecting power of judgment's own a priori and necessary heautonomous call. In the absence of its characteristic cognitive consequence of enabling "the judging of nature in accordance with empirical laws" (CJ, 5:412.14–15), that ordinarily subpersonal demand for an assumption of nature's inexistent order now no longer goes unnoticed. This is the point of a central but otherwise deeply enigmatic passage ahead of the deduction of judgments of taste – one of the rare passages in which Kant addresses the apriority of a priori reflecting judgments of purposiveness head-on. Kant there identifies heautonomy, so characteristic of the *subpersonal* operation of the transcendental principle of nature's purposiveness, as a signal feature also of singular aesthetic judgments. Kant notes that, in those judgments, the reflecting power of judgment "is for itself, subjectively, both object as well as law" (CJ, 5:288.25–26). But, unlike the subpersonal operation of the transcendental principle of the reflecting power of judgment, singular aesthetic judgments are an exercise of the reflecting power of judgment we are very much self-consciously aware of. In this way – and in those judgments – the heautonomy of the principle of nature's purposiveness accordingly itself attains a self-conscious cognitive role.

Now, this self-conscious awareness of the reflecting power of judgment's self-given self-governance is not merely a formal, somehow content-free echo of an underlying cognitive structure. It is, to the contrary, an awareness of the reflecting power of judgment's demand for an assumption of nature's purposiveness. But an awareness of being compelled to assume an origin in conceptual causality must be an awareness of being compelled to assume an origin in conceptual causality *of something or other*. Accordingly, on those occasions – and in those judgments – the reflecting power of judgment's demand for an assumption of nature's purposiveness is projected onto the empirical object in whose cognition the *saltus* in question is encountered.

The peculiar combination of epistemic apriority, logical singularity, and predicative holism accompanied by a quasi-auratic[89] sense of artifactuality that marks Kant's reflecting aesthetic and reflecting teleological judgments of purposiveness – and that appears so blatantly self-contradictory when seen through the familiar lens of conceptual determination – can now readily be explained as follows. First, the epistemic apriority of a priori reflecting judgments of purposiveness is the consequence of our awareness, in an encounter with nature's *saltūs*, of the reflecting power of judgment's self-given and self-governing a priori demand for a transcendentally necessary assumption of nature's inexistent conceptual order. Second, the logical singularity of a priori reflecting judgments of purposiveness is the consequence of our projection of that self-given and self-governing demand for an assumption of nature's inexistent conceptual order onto the object at hand. Third, the predicative holism of

---

[89] See note 18.

those judgments is the consequence of the fact that, qua demand for an assumption of that object's origin in its concept, it can only apply to the object "in the whole" (CJ, 5:377.11). Fourth, the quasi-auratic sense of artifactuality conveyed in such a reflecting judgment is the consequence of the fact that, qua cognitively necessitated but empirically ungrounded, nondetermining assumption, this predicative holism can only be manifest as a feeling of being unaccountably compelled to consider the object as "of conceptual origin."

In sum, an a priori reflecting judgment of purposiveness *just is* the reflecting power of judgment's self-given and self-governing demand to assume nature's inexistent conceptual order – attributed directly to a given empirical object: as the reflecting power of judgment's self-given and self-governing demand to assume its purposiveness.[90] Nor, of course, is there anything else it *could* be in the context of the third *Critique*. Depending on the adventitious absence or presence of post hoc generalizations about the sort of thing that triggers this cognitive projection, the respective judgment is then either an a priori reflecting judgment of a transcendental purposiveness *without* empirical purpose (and, hence, the kind of attribution of purposiveness that sets our cognitive faculties into a state of free, self-reinforcing, enjoyable play; or a judgment of beauty) or an a priori reflecting judgment of a transcendental purposiveness *with* empirical purpose (and, hence, the kind of attribution of purposiveness that issues in a fruitful and pronounced teleological loop; or a judgment of an organism).[91]

## 5.5 Out of the Box: Avoiding Critical Chaos

At the beginning of this Element, seeking to motivate Kant's idea that there is an unacknowledged a priori dimension peculiar to the life sciences, I noted that biological contexts do not call for (a posteriori) functional appraisal but that, to the contrary, (a priori) functional appraisal makes for biological contexts. One might wonder, however, why this purported a priori functional appraisal should be limited to biological contexts. Why should only biological nature strike us in this way? If, on occasion, we must estimate natural objects in functional terms as the result of a curious interplay between supersensible reality and a priori principles of cognition, then why should there not be natural but *non*organic beings we, on occasion, so appraise as well? And why should there not be organic beings we, on occasion, do not so appraise? And how, for that matter, do things begin and cease to be (required to be) appraised as organic beings? In short, how, on Kant's view, can we make sure that our functional appraisals attach to the *right* things?

---

[90] See CJ, 5:286.30–31, 287.04–07.    [91] See Section 2.2.6–7.

On one level, this question presupposes just what Kant's critical philosophy of biology seeks to disabuse us of: that there is a sensibly discernible or somehow independently intuitable property instantiated by organic beings. Ex hypothesi, any nonartifactual object that reliably served as a target of the reflecting power of judgment's self-given and self-governing demand to assume that object's purposiveness would be part of an organic world: a natural object that is and does what it is supposed to be and do. It would be an object in which "everything . . . must be considered as organized, and [in which] everything is also, in a certain relation to the thing itself, an organ in turn" (CJ, 5:377.21–23). To say that such a being might somehow be the "wrong" sort of thing to appraise in functional terms, or that it might somehow not be (sufficiently?) organic, would, on Kant's view, simply be confused.

At the same time, distinct empirical patterns (e.g., evolutionary, molecular, and morphological) are evidently characteristic of the organic sphere and form the basis of our scientific understanding of it. Those patterns appear to align fully with the purported a priori appraisals of that sphere. While this is no coincidence, at most it shows that a world in which entirely different empirical patterns fell within the scope of the organic would be a very different world from the one we inhabit. To say that it is no coincidence accordingly suggests that, for any world, sensible and supersensible nature are not two different natures but are two different dimensions of the same nature. To put the point more fully, the supersensible ground of conceptually determinable aspects of the organic world (reflected in our mechanistic assessments) and the supersensible ground of conceptually undeterminable aspects of the organic world (reflected in our teleological assessments) are not fundamentally different supersensible grounds. They are different ways in which aspects of the same supersensible ground come to be cognitively manifest – in determination and reflection, respectively.

As Kant puts it, the occasional necessity to judge products of nature teleologically – in supplementation of the universal necessity of judging all products of nature mechanistically – "leads to the necessity of a unification of both principles in the judging of things as natural purposes" (CJ, 5:414.1–3). And "the ground of this unifiability lies in that which is neither the one nor the other (neither mechanism nor connection to a purpose) but is the supersensible substratum of nature" (CJ, 5:414.28–30). In short, our different epistemic responses to the world are responses to the same world.

This, at long last, resolves the existential threat to Kant's transcendental philosophy of a fundamental inconsistency in a critical edifice that contains both a *Critique of Pure Reason* and a *Critique of the Power of Judgment*. This threat of "critical chaos" – or disorder at the level of critical philosophy itself – is at the heart of the "Antinomy of the Power of Judgment" (CJ, 5:385.04) in the teleological Dialectic. The threat arises because a *Critique of the Power of Judgment* whose transcendental teleological principle necessarily applies to at least some products of phenomenal nature appears to be in open conflict with the universal mechanism of the *Critique of Pure Reason*, so utterly foundational to Kant's critical project overall. In the antinomy, this conflict between determination and reflection plays out as a conflict between different interpretations of the scope of methodological mechanism: is mechanistic judging universally necessary and universally sufficient for the explanation of products of nature (thesis) or is it universally necessary but on occasion insufficient for the explanation of products of nature (antithesis)? The fundamental question of Kant's teleology (see Section 5.2), can thus be restated in this way: can – and how can – mechanistic judging and teleological judging on occasion be co-necessary?

The interaction of the heautonomy of the transcendental principle of nature's purposiveness with nature's *saltūs* explains how they can be. Teleological judgments of organized beings are nothing but the self-given and self-governing, subpersonal transcendental assumption of nature's determinability come to phenomenal awareness in the presence of aspects of supersensible reality (nature's *saltūs*) that, in principle, fail to support that assumption of determinability. The apriority and necessity of those judgments is, accordingly, of a very different nature than the apriority and necessity reflected in mechanistic judgments of the same objects. And yet, as Kant explains in the resolution of the antinomy in §78, both mechanistic and teleological judgments are rooted in the same "supersensible substratum of nature" (CJ, 5:414.30), if in different aspects thereof, respectively, those that support determinable *ectypoi* and those that do not. Since there is no contradiction in the idea of a supersensible ground harboring both, and since only mechanistic judgments are empirical determinations of the object at hand, there is then no contradiction in the conjoint necessity of judging the same appearance according to mechanistic and teleological principles at the same time.

More than registering a merely curious co-necessity, our a priori functional appraisals indicate that there is something exceedingly special about natural objects that instantiate the empirical patterns we associate with organic nature: a subterranean "unifiability" (CJ, 5:414.28) according to which neither these appraisals nor those patterns can float free of each other. In this bond beyond what can be determined empirically, there is then a glimpse also of nature's deeper systematic unity, a glimpse unavailable to any merely dogmatic insistence upon it. The poetic coda of the *Origin of Species* comes to mind: "There is a grandeur in this view of life" (Darwin, 1964, 490). This would make for an even more fitting conclusion to Kant's book than it is to Darwin's. After all, Kant presents an account of animate nature where Darwin does not. Kant explains how biological phenomena can be both "natural" and "purposes" – how the causal complexity of the natural world can strike us, on occasion, as the teleological complexity of a living world. Darwin's explanation? Divine exhalation.[92]

---

[92] "There is a grandeur in this view of life, with its several powers, having been *originally breathed* into a few forms or into one" (Darwin 1964, 425; my emphasis).

# References


Allison, H. E. (2001). *Kant's Theory of Taste*. Cambridge: Cambridge University Press.

(2003). "Kant's Antinomy of Teleological Judgment." In *Kant's Critique of the Power of Judgment: Critical Essays*, edited by Paul Guyer, 219–236. New York: Rowman & Littlefield.

Aristotle (1985). *The Complete Works of Aristotle: The Revised Oxford Translation*. 2 vols. Edited by Jonathan Barnes. Princeton: Princeton University Press.

Beck, L. W. (1978). "On the Putative Apriority of Judgments of Taste." In *Essays on Kant and Hume*, 167–170. New Haven: Yale University Press.

Benjamin, W. (1991). *Walter Benjamin: Gesammelte Schriften*. 7 vols. Edited by Rolf Tiedemann and Hermann Schweppenhäuser. Frankfurt am Main: Suhrkamp.

Bennett, J. (1974). *Kant's Dialectic*. Cambridge: Cambridge University Press.

Darwin, C. (1964). *On the Origin of Species*. Cambridge, MA: Harvard University Press.

Garson, J. (2016). *A Critical Overview of Biological Functions*. Berlin: Springer.

(2019). *What Biological Functions Are and Why They Matter*. Cambridge: Cambridge University Press.

Ginsborg, H. (1997). "Kant on Aesthetic and Biological Purposiveness." In *Reclaiming the History of Ethics: Essays for John Rawls*, edited by Andrews Reath, Barbara Herman, and Cristine Korsgaard, 329–360. Cambridge: Cambridge University Press.

(2001). "Kant on Understanding Organisms as Natural Purposes." In *Kant and the Sciences*, edited by Eric Watkins, 231–258. Oxford: Oxford University Press.

(2004). "Two Kinds of Mechanical Inexplicability in Kant and Aristotle." *Journal of the History of Philosophy* 42(1): 33–65.

(2006). "Thinking the Particular as Contained under the Universal." In *Aesthetics and Cognition in Kant's Critical Philosophy*, edited by Rebecca Kukla, 35–60. Cambridge: Cambridge University Press.

(2015). *The Normativity of Nature: Essays on Kant's* Critique of the Power of Judgment. Oxford: Oxford University Press.

Goy, I. (2017). *Kants Theorie der Biologie*. Berlin: De Gruyter.

Goy, I. and Watkins, E. (2014). "Introduction." In *Kant's Theory of Biology*, edited by Ina Goy and Eric Watkins, 1–22. Berlin: De Gruyter.

Grier, M. (1997). "Kant on the Illusion of a Systematic Unity of Knowledge." *History of Philosophy Quarterly* 14(9): 1–28.

Guyer, P. (1990). "Reason and Reflective Judgment: Kant on the Significance of Systematicity." *Noûs* 24: 17–43.

    (1997). *Kant and the Claims of Taste*. Cambridge: Cambridge University Press.

    (2000). "Editor's Introduction." In *Critique of the Power of Judgment*, edited by Paul Guyer, xiii–lii. Cambridge: Cambridge University Press.

    (2005). *Kant's System of Nature and Freedom*. Oxford: Oxford University Press.

    (2020). "'The Revised Method of Physico-theology': Kant's Reformed Teleology." In *Teleology: A History*, edited by Jeffrey K. McDonough, 186–218. Oxford: Oxford University Press.

Horstmann, R.-P. (1989). "Why Must There Be a Transcendental Deduction in Kant's *Critique of Judgment*?" In *Kant's Transcendental Deductions*, edited by Eckart Förster, 157–176. Stanford: Stanford University Press.

Hume, D. (1998). *Dialogues Concerning Natural Religion*. Indianapolis: Hackett.

Kant, I. (1902–). *Gesammelte Schriften*. 29 vols. Königlich Preussische Akademie der Wissenschaften. Berlin: G. Reimer.

    (1992). *Lectures on Logic: The Cambridge Edition of the Works of Immanuel Kant*. Edited and translated by J. Michael Young. Cambridge: Cambridge University Press.

    (1998). *Critique of Pure Reason: The Cambridge Edition of the Works of Immanuel Kant*. Edited and translated by Paul Guyer and Allen Wood. Cambridge: Cambridge University Press.

    (2000). *Critique of the Power of Judgment: The Cambridge Edition of the Works of Immanuel Kant*. Edited by Paul Guyer and translated by Paul Guyer and Eric Matthews. Cambridge: Cambridge University Press.

Kemp-Smith, N. (1992). *A Commentary to Kant's Critique of Pure Reason*. London: Macmillan.

Longuenesse, B. (1998). *Kant and the Capacity to Judge*. Princeton: Princeton University Press.

McDonough, J. (2011). "The Heyday of Teleology and Early Modern Philosophy." *Midwest Studies in Philosophy* XXXV: 179–204.

    (2020). "Not Dead Yet: Teleology and the 'Scientific Revolution.'" In *Teleology: A History*, edited by Jeffrey K. McDonough, 150–179. Oxford: Oxford University Press.

McLaughlin, P. (1990). *Kant's Critique of Teleology in Biological Explanation*. Lewiston: Edwin Mellen Press.

(2001). *What Functions Explain*. Cambridge: Cambridge University Press.

(2003). "Newtonian Biology and Kant's Mechanistic Concept of Causality." In *Kant's Critique of the Power of Judgment*, edited by Paul Guyer, 209–217. Oxford: Rowman & Littlefield.

Mensch, J. (2013). *Kant's Organicism*. Chicago: University of Chicago Press.

Messina, J. (2017). "Kant's Necessitation Account of Laws and the Nature of Natures." In *Kant and the Laws of Nature*, edited by Michela Massimi and Angela Breitenbach, 131–149. Cambridge: Cambridge University Press.

Neander, K. and Schulte, P. (1991). "Functions as Selected Effects: The Conceptual Analyst's Defense." *Philosophy of Science* 58: 168–184.

Neander, K. (2018). "Teleological Theories of Mental Content." *Stanford Encyclopedia of Philosophy*. Edited by Edward N. Zalta. https://plato.stanford.edu/archives/sum2022/entries/content-teleological.

Quarfood, M. (2004). *Transcendental Idealism and the Organism*. Stockholm Studies in Philosophy 26. Stockholm: Almqvist & Wiksell.

Schiller, F. (2003). "Kallias or Concerning Beauty: Letters to Gottfried Körner." Translated by Stefan Bird-Pollan. In *Classic and Romantic German Aesthetics*, edited by Jay Bernstein, 145–184. Cambridge: Cambridge University Press.

Schopenhauer, A. (1969). *The World as Will and Representation*. Translated by E. F. J. Payne. Garden City: Dover.

Teufel, T. (2011a). "Kant's *Non*-teleological Conception of Purposiveness." *Kant-Studien* 102(2): 232–252.

(2011b). "What Is the Problem of Teleology in Kant's 'Critique of the Teleological Power of Judgment'?" *SATS: Northern European Journal of Philosophy* 12(2): 198–236.

(2012). "What Does Kant Mean by 'Power of Judgment' in His *Critique of the Power of Judgment*?" *Kantian Review* 17(2): 297–326.

(2017). "Kant's Transcendental Principle of Purposiveness and the 'Maxim of the Lawfulness of Empirical Laws.'" In *Kant and the Laws of Nature*, edited by Michela Massimi and Angela Breitenbach, 108–127. Cambridge: Cambridge University Press.

(2023). "Teleological Power of Judgment: Dialectic." *The Kantian Mind*, edited by Sorin Baiasu and Marc Timmons, 260–271. New York: Routledge.

Watkins, E. (2009). "The Antinomy of Teleological Judgment." *Kant Yearbook* 1: 197–221.

(2019). *Kant on Laws*. Cambridge: Cambridge University Press.

Westphal, K. R. (2004). *Kant's Transcendental Proof of Realism*. Cambridge: Cambridge University Press.

Wolff, C. (1728). *Philosophia Rationalis Sive Logica* [LL]. *Praemittitur Discursus Praeliminaris De Philosophia in Genere*. Volume 2.1 of *Christian Wolff: Gesammelte Werke*, 1962–. Edited by Jean École, Hans Werner Arndt, Charles Anthony Corr, Joseph Ehrenfried Hofmann, and Marcel Thoman. Hildesheim: Georg Olms.

Zammito, J. (2006). "Teleology Then and Now: The Question of Kant's Relevance for Contemporary Controversies over Function in Biology." In *Kantian Teleology and the Biological Sciences*, edited by Joan Steigerwald, 748–770. *Studies in History and Philosophy of Science Part C: Studies in History and Philosophy of Biological and Biomedical Sciences* 37(4).

Zuckert, R. (2007). *Kant on Beauty and Biology*. Cambridge: Cambridge University Press.

# The Philosophy of Immanuel Kant

## Desmond Hogan
### *Princeton University*

Desmond Hogan joined the philosophy department at Princeton in 2004. His interests include Kant, Leibniz and German rationalism, early modern philosophy, and questions about causation and freedom. Recent work includes 'Kant on the Foreknowledge of Contingent Truths', *Res Philosophica* 91(1) (2014); 'Kant's Theory of Divine and Secondary Causation', in Brandon Look (ed.) *Leibniz and Kant*, Oxford University Press (2021); 'Kant and the Character of Mathematical Inference', in Carl Posy and Ofra Rechter (eds.) *Kant's Philosophy of Mathematics Vol. I*, Cambridge University Press (2020).

## Howard Williams
### *University of Cardiff*

Howard Williams was appointed Honorary Distinguished Professor at the Department of Politics and International Relations, University of Cardiff in 2014. He is also Emeritus Professor in Political Theory at the Department of International Politics, Aberystwyth University, a member of the Coleg Cymraeg Cenedlaethol (Welsh-language national college) and a Fellow of the Learned Society of Wales. He is the author of *Marx* (1980); *Kant's Political Philosophy* (1983); *Concepts of Ideology* (1988); *Hegel, Heraclitus and Marx's Dialectic* (1989); *International Relations in Political Theory* (1992); *International Relations and the Limits of Political Theory* (1996); *Kant's Critique of Hobbes: Sovereignty and Cosmopolitanism* (2003); *Kant and the End of War* (2012) and is currently editor of the journal Kantian Review. He is writing a book on the Kantian legacy in political philosophy for a new series edited by Paul Guyer.

## Allen Wood
### *Indiana University*

Allen Wood is Ward W. and Priscilla B. Woods Professor Emeritus at Stanford University. He was a John S. Guggenheim Fellow at the Free University in Berlin, a National Endowment for the Humanities Fellow at the University of Bonn and Isaiah Berlin Visiting Professor at the University of Oxford. He is on the editorial board of eight philosophy journals, five book series and The Stanford Encyclopedia of Philosophy. Along with Paul Guyer, Professor Wood is co-editor of The Cambridge Edition of the Works of Immanuel Kant and translator of the Critique of Pure Reason. He is the author or editor of a number of other works, mainly on Kant, Hegel and Karl Marx. His most recently published books are *Fichte's Ethical Thought*, Oxford University Press (2016) and *Kant and Religion*, Cambridge University Press (2020). Wood is a member of the American Academy of Arts and Sciences.

## About the Series

This Cambridge Elements series provides an extensive overview of Kant's philosophy and its impact upon philosophy and philosophers. Distinguished Kant specialists provide an up-to-date summary of the results of current research in their fields and give their own take on what they believe are the most significant debates influencing research, drawing original conclusions.

Printed by Integrated Books International,
United States of America